HIROSHIMA PEACE READER

By

Yoshiteru Kosakai

Translated By

Akira and Michiko Tashiro

Robert and Alice Ruth Ramseyer

Hiroshima Peace Culture Foundation

First edition, 1980
Second edition, 1983
Third edition, 1984
Fourth edition, 1985
Fifth edition, 1986
Sixth edition, 1988
Seventh edition, 1989
Published by the Hiroshima Peace Culture Foundation
1–5, Nakajima-cho, Naka-ku, Hiroshima 730, Japan
Printed by Keisuisha Co., Ltd., Hiroshima

FOREWORD

This book, *Hiroshima Peace Reader,* which is a brief description of the history of Hiroshima, the A-bomb and the Memorial Peace Park, is published by the Hiroshima Peace Culture Foundation.

The booklet consists of three chapters. The first chapter deals with the history of Hiroshima beginning with the Mōri era. It concludes with a description of the city which rose from the ashes as a phoenix after the A-bombing, the city which has been rebuilt as an international peace city. The second chapter is mainly concerned with the disaster of the atomic bomb. In the third chapter the historical background of the Peace Memorial Park and the monuments built in and around the park are described in detail with an attached map showing the location of monuments.

This book was written by Mr. Yoshiteru Kosakai, chief editor of the Hiroshima City Historical Collective as well as director of the Hiroshima City Archives Library. The photographic materials were obtained through the cooperation of the Hiroshima Municipal Library, the Hiroshima Peace Memorial Museum, and the Chūgoku Press. To all of these I wish to express my deep gratitude. Mr. Kosakai died on January 2, 1986. Since that time this book has been revised by the staff of this foundation.

I hope this booklet will be useful in many fields in learning about HIROSHIMA.

Takeshi Araki

T. Araki

President, Hiroshima
Peace Culture Foundation

Contents

Chapter 1

History of Hiroshima

Portrait of
Terumoto Mōri

The Construction of a Castle by the Mōri Family

The history of Hiroshima as a castle town began when Terumoto Mōri left Kōriyama Castle in Yoshida, Takata County, and built a castle on the shores of Hiroshima Bay.

On April 15, 1589, Terumoto appointed Naritatsu Ninomiya and Motokiyo Hoita magistrates in charge of construction and ordered them to begin the foundation work with all possible speed. The next year the castle town was laid out, the moat dug, and the castle buildings themselves were under construction. Castle construction proceeded even though during that year Terumoto was on duty protecting Kyoto, while Hideyoshi Toyotomi was attacking Odawara Castle. With the fall of Odawara Castle he was able to leave Kyoto, and on January 8, 1591, he made a grand entrance into his new castle which had been completed except for a small area of stonework.

At that time, Niho, Eba, and Ujina (presently Motoujina) were islands in the shallow bay. Earth and sand, washed down the Ōta River, accumulated in the bay over a long period of time and formed a number of flat islands. At that time people began to occupy these islands and called the area "Gokaura" or "Gokashō" or "Gokason" (Five Villages). Some say that the name of Hiroshima came from the fact that the castle was built on the largest of the islands. (Hiro means wide; shima means island.)

Hiroshima Castle is also called "Rijō" (the Castle of the Carp). This is because "Koi" in Koi-ura, the whole area where the castle was located, is a homonym of carp in Japanese.

The Mōris had their first contact with Hiroshima when the Kamakura shogunate appointed them lords of Yoshida in Takata County. Steadily extending their influence over the area, they wanted a foothold on the coast for both economic and military reasons.

Since commercial traffic on the Seto Inland Sea was then under the control of the Ōuchi family and commerce on the Sea of Japan north of Hiroshima was controlled by the Amako family, the Mōris were in an insecure position. However, during the time of Motonari, Terumoto's grandfather, they transferred their allegiance from the Amakos to the Ōuchis, who gave them land in Kabe, Fukawa-Kami·Shimo, Nukushina and Ku-mura. Furthermore, Motonari advanced south along the Ōta River. He collided with the Takeda Clan based in Kanayama Castle (Gion-chō), who were responsible for the Province of Aki (the greater part of the present Hiroshima Prefecture); with the Amako Clan, who were allied with the Takedas; and with the priestly family which ruled Itsukushima. Motonari conquered these rulers one after the other and as a result of the fall of the Takedas, the Ōuchis entrusted him with their former lands. Motonari now had the land on the shore of Hiroshima Bay which he had wanted.

Portrait of Motonari Mōri

In 1555, Motonari defeated Harukata Sue who had betrayed Yoshitaka Ōuchi and forced him to commit suicide. After that, he subjugated two domains of Bōchō (presently a part of Yamaguchi Prefecture) and united the whole Chūgoku district under his sway. Plans for Terumoto to build Hiroshima Castle were probably made during the days of Motonari.

With the completion of the castle, as the retainers moved in from Yoshida, merchants and artisans were recruited from many places. Thus, a new castle town, befitting a great feudal lord, was born. Gokason, which had been nothing more than tiny fishing villages among the reeds suddenly became a bustling town. Bridges and roads were then constructed, including the Motoyasu Bridge, the Honkawa Bridge, and the road running in front of the castle from east to west connecting Horikawa-chō, Hirataya-chō, Nakajima-hon-machi (presently in the Peace Park), and Sakaimachi. The Sanyō highway which had run north of Gokason now ran through the town.

Hiroshima Castle (prewar)

Rivers running through the town were utilized for water transport, connecting the town with the Seto Inland Sea. Tenjin-chō (east of the Peace Park) on the Motoyasu River, then called Funa-machi, had a flourishing wharf. In addition, two canals were built, the Hirataya in the east, and the Seitō (over which the Takano Bridge was built) in the west, to serve as harbors. Onomichi-chō, Shioya-chō, Nishiuoya-chō, Horikawa-chō, Higashiuoya-chō and Shinsenba (Funaba)-chō developed along these canals. They have since been filled in and are now used as roads.

On the other hand, there were also medieval market traders. At Tōka-ichi-chō in the west, there was a regular market for vegetables, fruits, and processed farm products such as straw mats, tatami mats, and baskets made of bamboo, brought in from places on the upper courses of the Ōta River. Tōkaichi itself was said to have been a market place transferred from Yoshida, and the regular market days were very busy.

These traditional neighborhood names, established during the days of the Mōris, the Fukushimas and the Asanos, were retained until the community reorganization which followed the devastation of the atomic bombing.

After the death of Hideyoshi Toyotomi on August 18, 1598, Ieyasu Tokugawa began to extend his power. Terumoto Mōri, commander-in-chief of the opposing western army, was defeated by the Tokugawa forces at the battle of Sekigahara, and forced to withdraw into the two domains of Bōchō (present Yamaguchi Prefecture). Thus he only had ten years as lord of Hiroshima Castle.

Entry of Masanori Fukushima into Hiroshima

After the Mōris had left Hiroshima, Masanori Fukushima, who had taken the side of the Tokugawa at the battle of Sekigahara, arrived as governor-general of Geishū and Bishū (present Hiroshima Prefecture). He came from Kiyosu Castle in Owari (present Aichi Prefecture). As the Fukushimas' reign began, Hiroshima developed rapidly. Communities were organized under magistrates, neighborhood groups were set up to control the populace, and each group had an appointed senior leader. This system lasted for over 260 years until the Meiji Restoration.

Portrait of Masanori Fukushima

The expansion of the city area was also promoted and the following areas were developed: Kannon-Shinkai which covers most of the present Kanon-machi area, Kirishitan-Shinkai which is the present Takeya-chō-Fujimi-chō area, Kokutaiji-Shinkai which is the present Kokutaiji-chō, Roku-chōme-Shinkai, Kakomachi-Shinkai, Funairi-Shinkai and the eastern and southern parts of Hijiyama.

The Fukushimas endeavored to improve the domain by carrying out a land survey. However, they were moved to Tsugaru (present Aomori Prefecture) in Ōshū (Tōhoku district) because they had Hiroshima Castle, which was damaged by a flood in 1619, repaired without permission from the Tokugawa Feudal Government. The rule of the Fukushimas lasted for only about 20 years.

The Asano Rule

On August 8, 1619, Nagaakira Asano entered Hiroshima from Wakayama in Kishū (a part of the present Kinki district) replacing the Fukushimas. The Asanos, close allies of the Tokugawa rulers, were installed as the key to Tokugawa control of the Chūgoku district and with lands assessed at 426,000 koku of rice, they ruled for 250 years until the time of the Meiji Restoration. Under Asano rule the city continued to grow and prosper.

Portrait of Nagaakira Asano

Like the Fukushimas, the Asanos added new areas to the city. According to a map drawn in the Kansei period (1789–1800), new land was added beyond the newly developed Kirishitan addition. In the same way there was newly filled-in land added to the Hijiyama and Roku-chōme additions. Progress in filling in shallow areas of the bay to create new land was as dramatic as the leveling of mountains to create new housing areas today.

Besides these, quite a few newly developed areas, large and small, are recorded on old maps drawn about that time. In this way, Hijiyama, Nihoshima, and Eba, originally islands, became part of the mainland.

During the Asano period, there were almost no military disturbances. In parallel with the development of a rich samurai culture, the culture of the townspeople, with their increased economic strength, also made rapid progress. As the Tokugawa regime promoted Confucianism, the lords of the Asano Clan gave important positions to Confucian scholars. For example, they invited Jōzan Ishikawa from Kyoto. In 1725, a school exclusively for the children of clansmen was established in Hakushima and the establishment of private schools and temple schools was encouraged. With these educational policies, a rich culture began to bloom.

Sanyō Rai, a son of Shunsui Rai who was a Confucian scholar serving the Asano Clan, helped to develop the ideas which led to the Meiji Restoration. His book the *Nihongaishi* (an Unofficial History

Portrait of Sanyō Rai

of Japan) left a deep impression on the minds of people at that time. He was also a distinguished poet. There are still many people who love to recite his poems.

The Meiji Restoration

The visit of the American mission under Perry in 1853 undermined the Tokugawa regime which had kept Japan closed to foreign influence, and stimulated the people to look in new directions. As the political situation grew strained, the Asano, as an influential clan of the Chūgoku district, rapidly rose to a higher political position.

As the feudal rulers of Japan, divided between those who wanted to preserve the status quo and those who insisted on change, engaged in heated controversy, the intervention of the traditional nobility in the Imperial Court moved the focus of political activity from Edo (Tokyo) to Kyoto. In the midst of these rapid changes in the political situation, the strength of the Tokugawa Regime gradually weakened. At the same time, such influential clans as the Satsuma-han (the Shimazus), the Chōshū-han (the Mōris) and the Tosa-han (the Yamanouchis) rapidly gained in strength. Among them, the Chōshū-han took the lead in the movement to overthrow the Tokugawa Regime with the slogan, "Revere the Emperor! Expel the Barbarians." They had the backing of the Imperial Court, the traditional nobility, and many young samurai. It is said that the Mōris led the movement in order to pay off old scores – their defeat at the battle of Sekigahara.

Some clans were displeased that the Chōshū-han had made such a spectacular advance into the central government. The Satsuma and the Aizu-han working together succeeded in expelling the Chōshū-han. However, the Chōshū-han marched on Kyoto in an attempt to regain power, and finally staged the "Kinmon-no-Hen." Because of this incident, it was called "the Emperor's enemy."

The Last Years of the Hiroshima-han

In 1864, the subjugation of Chōshū was undertaken by the combined forces of the Tokugawa Regime and the anti-Tokugawa clans. Ordered to lead the attack on Chōshū, the Hiroshima-han became the focus of political concern. The Tokugawa officials, and the armies of each clan entered Hiroshima which had become a base for the whole army. Although the situation was critical, peace was restored without a battle when the Chōshū-han apologized and beheaded three of its leaders. The heads of the three were examined at the Kokutai Temple in Hiroshima (moved to Koi Pass in 1977) and the attack was called off. However, some of the lower warriors in Chōshū who were dissatisfied with this settlement organized an attack force of farmers and townsmen with arms imported from England. They concluded a secret agreement with the Satsuma-han to further intensify the movement for overthrowing the Shogunate. Knowing of this movement, the Shogunate was determined to subjugate the Chōshū-han. However the clans, in financial difficulty, could not meet the Tokugawa orders to dispatch troops. The Tokugawa Regime no longer held power as in the past, and rapid changes in the world were bringing about the breakdown of feudalism.

Inspection gate in Hiroshima during the period of social turmoil at the end of the Edo Era

Hiroshima became a military base for the Tokugawa Regime with the possibility of becoming a dangerous battle field, however, the Hiroshima-han had opposed military action to subjugate the Chōshū-han and devoted its energies to mediating between the Shogunate and the Chōshū-han.

On the death of Iemochi on July 20, 1866, Yoshinobu Hitotsubashi succeeded as Shogun. Since he saw that the war was not going in his favor, he stopped the attempt to subjugate Chōshū. With this, the powerlessness of the Tokugawa Regime was revealed to the whole country, and the political situation took a sudden turn from restoring power to the Tokugawa Regime to the establishment of imperial rule. At a meeting held at the Kyoto Imperial Palace in December, 1867, the group who wanted to overthrow the Shogunate by force of arms had a heated argument with the group supporting the Tosa-han that wanted to settle the situation peacefully. However, the Hiroshima-han arbitrated between the two parties, and nation-wide fighting was avoided.

Establishment of the Meiji Government

Although the Battle of Toba-Fushimi (the Boshin War) and other battles were provoked by discontented vassals of the Shogun, they ended in the total defeat of the Shogun's forces. In 1868, the new Meiji government was formed. With the inauguration of the new government, the system of the administration of local municipalities was also changed.

In July, 1871, the feudal clan system was abolished and the Hiroshima fief became Hiroshima Prefecture. The castle town of Hiroshima began the process of rebirth as one of the most important cities of Japan.

Outbreak of Rioting

On the pretext of deterring Nagamichi Asano, the former lord, from moving his residence to Tokyo when the rule of feudal clans was abolished and prefectures established, a large-scale riot was started throughout the prefecture. Known in history as the Buichi Riot, it was an explosion of the uncertainty which the simple farmers felt toward the new government, and of dissatisfaction with the ruling class. Buichiro (coming from Arita Village in Yamagata County), the leader of the riot, and 24 others were executed.

Hiroshima Becomes a City

In April, 1872, the system of local administration was completely changed. The old towns and villages were abolished and the entire country was divided into large districts and subdivided into smaller ones. The town of Hiroshima was one large district subdivided into 4 small districts. Large districts were administered by officers called kochō and fuku kochō. Small districts also had administrative officers. Hiroshima officially became a city on April 1, 1889, under the new system of municipalities. A physician, Akira Miki, was appointed the first mayor. The population at that time was 83,387. On September 21 of that year the new city hall was opened on the site of the grain warehouse of the Hiroshima-han in Nakajima-shin-machi (Peace Boulevard). This was the center of municipal administration for 39 years until 1928 when the present city hall was opened in Kokutaiji-chō.

Construction of Ujina Harbor

For some ten years before and after the birth of Hiroshima City, there were major projects and events which determined the direction of Hiroshima as a city. The construction of Ujina Harbor was one of these. Although there had long been a plan to develop a new area on Ujina Bay, objections were raised against it by former warriors who were opposed to the misuse of funds appropriated for their rehabilitation when clans were abolished, and by fishermen who feared losing their fishing grounds. The prefectural governor, Sadaaki Senda who assumed office in 1880, was enthusiastic about the construction of Ujina Harbor and successfully talked them into agreement. And on September 5, 1884, the ground-breaking ceremony was held. The harbor was nearly completed in November, 1889, at a total cost of more than 300,000 yen, which was several times as much as the original estimate. With this construction work, the sea from the Minami-Shinkai

Bronze statue of Baron Sadaaki Senda (Ujina Miyuki-dōri)

southward to Ujina Island was reclaimed forming 2,076,442m2 of new land.

Ujina Harbor was built to serve as a water gateway (commercial port), which would ensure the prosperity of Hiroshima.

The Opening of the Sanyō Railway

On June 10, 1894, the Sanyō Railway which had been opened as far as Itozaki, was extended to Hiroshima. Hiroshima Station, as a land gateway, was built in Higashi-Matsubara in Ōsuga Village. A month later, when the Sino-Japanese War broke out, Hiroshima Station and Ujina Harbor became very important for military transportation. The construction of a military railway (the Ujina Line) between the station and the harbor was started on the day after war broke out. It was completed in only 16 days.

In September, 1897, the Sanyō Railway was extended westward to Tokuyama. Both Yokogawa and Koi stations were constructed at that time. The Kure Line was opened in 1903 because of military necessity. The Kabe Line (operated by the Great Japan Railway Corporation) was built in 1910 and the Geibi Line (operated by the Geibi Railway Corporation) in 1915. Thus train transportation superseded shipping on the Ōta River.

The Formation of Hiroshima as a Military City

The Meiji Restoration provided the opportunity for the castle town of Hiroshima to be reborn as an economic and cultural city. However, as the Meiji Government pursued its policy of strengthening the military, it soon became apparent that Hiroshima, at the center of the Chūgoku district with a good harbor, was ideally situated for military purposes.

After the abolition of clans and the establishment of prefectures, the first detached garrison of Western Japan was set up in the Hiroshima Castle. In 1873, the Hiroshima garrison of the Fifth Military District, one of six garrisons in the entire nation, was established to govern Hiroshima and nine other prefectures. Thus Hiroshima again became a military city. When the 11th Regiment of Infantry was organized, its units were stationed in Hiroshima. In 1886, the Hiroshima garrison was renamed the Fifth Division. New military installations were built one after another not only in the castle but also outside the castle, steadily strengthening Hiroshima as an army base.

The Sino-Japanese War and the Russo-Japanese War

When the Sino-Japanese War broke out in August, 1894, the Fifth Division was the first to be sent to the front. They were followed by soldiers from all over Japan, leaving Ujina Harbor daily for active service overseas. Ujina Harbor was very busy with many military transports coming and going.

On September 15, the Meiji Emperor moved Imperial Headquarters to the Hiroshima Castle where he planned strategy. An extraordinary session of the Imperial Diet was held in the provisional Diet building built in a corner of the west drill ground (around the site of the Hiroshima Castle) with civil and military officials accompanying the Emperor.

Provisional Diet Building

Hiroshima looked as if it were the capital. Until the Emperor left Hiroshima on April 27, 1895, the city was unprecedentedly prosperous and busy, with high government officials coming and going, soldiers leaving for the front, the reception of wounded soldiers, and tradespeople and workers coming from all over Japan.

The war brought more people to Hiroshima, and resulted in the expansion of military installations. Thus Hiroshima made rapid progress as one of the important military cities of Japan.

In 1904, as the Russo-Japanese War broke out, Hiroshima was again brought to the fore as a large-scale army base of operations.

Former Imperial Headquarters

Through these wars, the industrial economy of Hiroshima took great strides and the establishment of stock exchanges, banks, and industries was promoted. Hiroshima became an economic city as well as a military city. It also had the appearance of an educational city equipped with a number of educational facilities.

Hiroshima, secure in its position as a military city, became more populous and prosperous as wars and incidents occurred throughout the Meiji and Taisho periods. Therefore, Hiroshima was not so influenced by the cutback in armaments during the 1920s.

The Greater East Asia War

Along with expansion of its rule as a military city, Hiroshima became remarkably modernized.

After the Manchurian Incident, the Shanghai Incident and the China Incident, the Japanese army and navy attacked Pearl Harbor in Hawaii and launched an attack on the northern Malay Peninsula on December 8, 1941. Japan rushed into the Greater East Asia War (the Pacific War) at one stroke. In Hiroshima, a center of military affairs since the Sino-Japanese and the Russo-Japanese Wars, military installations were expanded and various heavy industries were rapidly developed.

In 1942, a Marine headquarters (under the command of Lieutenant General Bunrō Saeki) was set up in Ujina, and related units were arranged on the coast around Hiroshima City. Later on when the atomic bomb was dropped, these units, located about 4 kilometers away from the city, were saved from destruction. They sent out relief squads and took a very active part in aiding the wounded, clearing the dead bodies and cleaning the streets.

Preparations for the Decisive Battle on the Mainland

After the outbreak of the war, the air defense setup of the city was rapidly strengthened and was much stricter than in other cities. However, after Japan, which had been victorious in the early stages of the war, lost the battle of Guadalcanal in 1943, the military situation grew steadily worse, and it appeared that the mainland of Japan would be turned into a battlefield. The army hurriedly prepared for a decisive battle on the mainland. With these preparations Hiroshima was to take on a new role. Japan was divided into two parts; the First General Headquarters was placed in Tokyo, and the Second General Headquarters (under the command of Marshal Shunroku Hata) in Hiroshima, where the headquarters of the Chūgoku District Governor-General (led by Korekio Ōtsuka), the highest administrative body, commissioned by the central government was also established.

In 1944, the U.S. forces occupied Saipan, the last strategic point of the Japanese army on the south Pacific front, and established an air base from which to attack the mainland of Japan. In November full-scale air raids were begun, devastating the cities of Japan one after the other.

Under such conditions, Hiroshima City began the evacuation of students above the third grade of elementary school and of other citizens whose presence was not essential. With the threat of incendiary bombings, demolition of buildings to make fire lanes was carried out on a wide scale. For the demolition of buildings, volunteer army corps in various places, organized according to the National Volunteer Army Conscription Law, and mobilized students of various middle schools and girls' schools were gathered to engage in the work each day.

An evacuation plan for the citizens was made in preparation for the outbreak of a major conflagration caused by the air raids. The evacuation location of each neighborhood association was specified in advance in order to avoid confusion. The evacuation of people that had been organized at the outset of the air raids was prohibited at the end of the war in order to secure personnel necessary for air defense.

Demolition of Hiroshima

On August 6, 1945, with one Atomic Bomb, almost all of the houses and buildings in Hiroshima were instantly destroyed. They immediately caught fire and were reduced to ashes. In the case of wooden houses, those which were within 1 kilometer of the hypocenter were literally broken into pieces at the moment of the explosion. Those ranging between 1 kilometer and 2 kilometers from the hypocenter were completely destroyed. Those ranging 2 to 3 kilometers were severely damaged. Even the houses 3 to 4 kilometers away from the center of the explosion were badly damaged.

Fire-ravaged area

In the case of reinforced concrete buildings, those which were near the center of the explosion had their roofs collasped. Some of the buildings were flattened and became piles of rubble.

After destruction by the violent blast and pressure caused by the explosion came a fierce fire. Every building within 1 kilometer of the hypocenter was totally destroyed by the fire whether it was wooden or reinforced concrete. The buildings located 1 to 2 kilometers from the center were mostly destroyed by the fire, and those 2 to 3 kilometers from the center were partly destroyed.

Hiroshima Prefectural Government Hall, which was a wooden building 900 meters from the hypocenter, was knocked down and burned. Hiroshima City Hall (1.2 kilometers from the center) also caught fire and the entire building was gutted, although the main shell of the Hall which was reinforced concrete was left standing.

Mayor Awaya died at his home and a great many officials were killed in their offices. The A-bomb destroyed all levels of administration, transportation facilities including railroads, the communication system, journalism, offices and factories of private and bublic corporations, and all other facilities. The total destruction of these facilities caused such great confusion that it was utterly impossible to grasp the number of the dead and wounded.

Needless to say, army troops deployed around Hiroshima Castle, which was the center of Hiroshima as a military city, were nearly annihilated. On the evening of August 6, Vice Inspector General Hattori of the Chūgoku District Superintendent's Office, Director of Hiroshima Prefectural Police Ishihara, and Governer Takano, who had returned from a business trip, gathered at Tamon-in Temple at the entrance of Hijiyama Park. They formed both a Temporary Prefectural Government Office and a Temporary Air-defence Headquarters. It was only thirteen hours later that they reported the disastrous situation and asked for help from the Central Government and other related organizations. Therefore the relief activities on the very day of the explosion were only carried out by the Akatsuki Corps sent from Ujina, naval personnel sent from the Naval Base at Kure, and a few small hospitals which survived the disaster.

Life in the Burnt-out City

About a month after the A-bomb was dropped, the temporary first-aid stations established in hospitals and schools around the city, gradually returned to normalcy. Those citizens who had evacuated to the suburbs began to come back one by one to the city, which had become a wide stretch of burnt-out ruins. They built shacks made of tin sheets dug out of the ruins and started life again. However, having returned to the city, they were thrown into a state of lethargy since there were no companies or factories to employ them; there was not enough food to eat, and they were worried about developing A-bomb diseases. Just then, a typhoon hit the city. It raged from the middle of the night on September 17 to the next morning. The burnt city was completely submerged and the air raid shelters and shacks, in which the A-bomb survivors lived, were destroyed. The people were hard hit, losing their place to sleep and what little belongings they had. Quite a few of them gave up living in the city and went back to the countryside again.

Shacks around Yokogawa Station (taken in mid-October 1945 by Shunkichi Kikuchi, photo courtesy of the Chūgoku Newspaper Company)

After the typhoon had passed, it suddenly became autumnlike. Beautiful weather continued for some time and green grass started to grow here and there in the burnt city. The grass was horseweed, which grew as tall as a man. Using the horseweed as a main ingredient, dumplings were made and sold in Eba and other areas which had remained unburnt. People who could not go on with an empty stomach any longer ate them to relieve their hunger, though they were unappetizing.

According to foreign news dispatches, Hiroshima, contaminated by radioactivity, would be barren for the next 70 years and no one would be able to live there. However, finding green grass starting to grow all over, hibakusha (the A-bomb survivors) were given new hope for life.

Around the middle of September, elementary school children who had been evacuated returned to the city and schools were reopened in the burnt-out shells of ferroconcrete buildings. However, many classes were held outside and there were no teaching materials. Moreover the children could not concentrate on studying because of their empty stomachs. Among those children there were some who had lost their houses, parents and brothers and sisters. Some of them were eventually either put in the custody of relatives living at a distance or adopted.

Around that time, black-market stalls were opened by discharged soldiers and citizens of other countries along the streets where people gathered in front of Hiroshima Station, and were doing a good business. However, many hibakusha could not afford to buy goods there. They had to start self-sufficient vegetable gardens around their shacks after clearing away the rubble. Seedlings and seeds were either supplied by the city office or given by their acquaintances living in the countryside.

Winter in the burnt-out city was the severest one they had had in recent years. In this freezing cold weather, hibakusha made fires with the unburnt pieces of wood they had raked up. With this scanty heat they warmed themselves and managed to survive.

Out of the Ashes

The reconstruction of Hiroshima began with relief activities, mainly by the army (the Akatsuki Unit), immediately after the bombing. They removed the countless dead bodies in the first four or five days, cleared the principal roads for truck traffic, and of course helped to house and treat the wounded.

Since the war was still going on, it was urgent to restore the functions of the important military bases. Emergency measures were taken to restore communications, electricity, and transportation.

As the army, which had been the main force in the reconstruction work, was disbanded at the end of the war, the work stagnated. The city government, almost totally destroyed by the bombing, was not capable of taking over the reconstruction work. It was forced to depend heavily on aid from the prefectural governments of Hiroshima and neighboring prefectures. Through the relief work of the groups sent by these prefectures, Hiroshima City gradually began to grope its way back to life.

Image of the Future City On February 22, 1946, Governor Kusunose invited a number of leaders to the prefectural office for a round-table discussion on the reconstruction and future of Hiroshima. The following is a summary of the statements of each person present.

Governor Kusunose:

I prefer the word reconstruction to restoration. There are two aspects of reconstruction. One is short-term reconstruction, such as running streetcars, building bridges and temporary houses as quickly as possible. The other is long-term reconstruction, which can not be carried out soon because of the present shortage of building materials. We need to work on it step by step. How about collecting drawings of reconstruction plans for Hiroshima from people all over the world?

Yoshirō Saeki (religious historian):

I'm opposed to the idea of building Hiroshima as a large city. A small Hiroshima is good enough, but it should be perfectly constructed as a city. The present state of metropolitan Tokyo is a result of the failure of party politics. Such a situation should be avoided. I think that we should permit Hiroshima as a metropolitan center to grow in a natural way.

Yōko Ōta (novelist):

The banks of the rivers of Hiroshima should become green areas and parks. Constructing apartments on the outskirts of the city is an urgent need in order to provide living facilities for the A-bomb victims who are now compelled to live in shacks. Many trees should be planted in the city. I would like to interweave dream and reality in harmony and enrich the citizens' lives.

Tomiko Kōra (deputy mayor of Kure City):

I want to keep the vast expanse of the burnt-out area intact as a memorial graveyard for the sake of ever-lasting world peace. I have doubts about building a city on the place where countless numbers of people have died. It is not necessary to build the new Hiroshima on its old site. I think that we should search for a new place in the suburbs and construct the new Hiroshima there.

Hikojirō Ōshio (head of the broadcasting department of the Hiroshima Broadcasting Company):

Presently I feel strongly that we need to improve the level of culture. I would like to see a library constructed soon even if it is just a shack. Also movie theaters and playhouses should be built as soon as possible to meet the needs of citizens who are hungry for culture.

Mr. Hayashi (assistant abbot of the Hiroshima Betsuin):

The delay in reconstruction comes because a comprehensive city plan has not been announced yet. The routes of the main roads at least should be decided at once. Temples should be scattered one in each community instead of clustering them in one area as they were before the war. Then they could be utilized by the local people for various activities, serving as community auditoriums.

Yoshirō Fukui (artist):

I would like to see wide roads constructed and green belts built along the riversides. I want to see Hiroshima become a modern city displaying the highest quality of original Japanese culture.

The outline of the opinions expressed above shows much enthusiasm among the citizens for the reconstruction of Hiroshima as a peaceful modern city full of green vegetation. However, at that time, these opinions were considered a fantastic dream.

In the summer of 1946, in the outskirts of the burnt-out area, Danbara and Niho in the east, Ujina and Eba in the south, Koi, Kōgo and Kusatsu in the west, Misasa-hon-machi 4-chōme and Ōshiba in the north, the population increased rapidly because there was an influx of people who fled the city at the time of the bombing, demobilized soldiers, and repatriates from the mainland of China and Korea. Though various shops and recreational facilities in temporary wooden buildings started to appear, the completely burnt-out areas remained empty except for a few places, such as the areas in front of Hiroshima Station, Matoba-chō, Yokogawa and Koi, where black markets were thriving. The nearer one approached the hypocenter, the more vacant lots remained where horseweeds grew thickly.

Peace Restoration Festival/Restoration Bureau

On August 6, 1946, the first anniversary of the bombing, the Hiroshima Peace Restoration Festival was held in the precincts of the Hiroshima Gokoku Shrine (near the present baseball stadium) amidst tears by the surviving citizens of the city. They prayed for the peace of the souls of the A-bomb victims and pledged themselves to the restora-

Peace Restoration Festival (taken on August 5, 1946 by Toshio Kawamoto, photo courtesy of the Chūgoku Newspaper Company)

tion of world peace. With the flags of each neighborhood association in front, four to five thousand citizens gathered carrying flags draped in black and banners on whicn the slogan "World peace begins from Hiroshima" was written. Being under Allied occupation, government agencies could not sponsor such a festival. In addition, permission to hold a festival had to be granted by the General Headquarters of the Occupation Forces in Tokyo and its branch in Kure. The festival was carried out under Occupation surveillance and no anti-American speeches or actions were permitted.

Exactly at 8:15 on August 6, sirens were sounded all over the city. Street cars, buses and people all stopped and those in offices stood up, leaving their pens and abacuses on their desks. Then they paid silent tribute to the victims for one minute. This first anniversary Peace Restoration Festival was of deep significance. It gave people, crushed by privations, a flash of hope, which heightened their desire for restoration of the city.

The city made a basic plan for restoration and carried it forward by starting the Restoration Bureau in January, 1946, and organizing the Restoration Council in February in the burnt-out city hall. The plan to build the Peace Boulevard (100-meter-wide avenue) was also made at that time. Though administrative agencies and the citizens of Hiroshima had very strong enthusiasm for the plan, it was extremely difficult to carry it out since the damage done by the A-bomb was so complete and because Japan was under military occupation. The hibakusha had not recovered their physical strength and had no energy to engage in the restoration of their city, living, as many did, in wretched hovels which did not even shelter them from rain. It was only around 1949 or 1950 that they resumed some semblance of normal living.

Inauguration of a Mayor Elected by Popular Vote

In April, 1947, Shinzō Hamai was elected mayor by popular vote in the first post-war election. Hiroshima was newly born on the principle of democracy.

Mayor Hamai, hoping to make Hiroshima the Mecca of all people who long for world peace, established the Hiroshima Peace Memorial Service Committee and decided to hold the Peace Memorial Ceremony on August 6 every year. He also decided to issue a Peace Declaration.

The First Peace Memorial Ceremony

On August 6, 1947, the first Peace Memorial Ceremony was held in an open area in Jisenji-no-hana (This area is now included in the Peace Park). The ceremony took place around a wooden peace tower which was built for the occasion. After a silent prayer by the people present, the Peace Bell was rung. Then Mayor Hamai took the platform and read aloud to the world the first Peace Declaration. "These fearful weapons have made us face the revolutionary concept of the inevitability and necessity of ever-lasting peace. That is to say, these weapons have made the people of the world recognize clearly that a war, fought with nuclear weapons, would mean the annihilation of human beings and the end of civilization. This must lead us to the realization of unconditional peace and to the birth of a new way of life and a new world." Mayor Hamai expressed his convictions eloquently, speaking from his own experience as a hibakusha.

This annual Peace Memorial Ceremony has stirred interest throughout the world. Each year many sympathizers send encouraging and supporting words to the Hiroshima city government.

"No More Hiroshimas" Movement

Rev. Kiyoshi Tanimoto of Nagarekawa Church, a hibakusha, was interviewed in Tokyo by a United Press correspondent, Lutherford Poats in 1948 and the interview appeared in the *Stars and Stripes,* the newspaper of the American armed forces. In this article Poats used a new expression "No More Hiroshimas", which was reprinted in other American newspapers. Alfred Parker, custodian of Tenth Avenue Baptist Church, Oakland, California, was struck by this message and immediately proposed a "No More Hiroshimas" movement to people of 26 countries.

Mayor Hamai reading the Peace Declaration (August 6, 1948. Photo courtesy of the Chūgoku Newspaper Company)

With this as a beginning, people all over the world became interested in the movement, and "Hiroshima Day" meetings were held on August 6 in many parts of the world.

Mayor Hamai, in the second Peace Memorial Ceremony in 1948, read his Peace Declaration: "I pray from the bottom of my heart that No More Hiroshimas will be created on this earth." His words were translated into English and written on the Peace Tower in huge letters. Thus he expressed his determination to make Hiroshima a Mecca for world peace.

Peace Memorial City Hiroshima

Peace Memorial Ceremony (August 6, 1948. Photo courtesy of the Chūgoku Newspaper Company)

Hiroshima is no longer merely a Japanese city. It has become recognized throughout the world as a Mecca of world peace. From this standpoint, Mayor Hamai felt that the reconstruction of Hiroshima should be initiated by the Japanese Government and in that way the new peaceful Japan could gain credibility with foreign countries. The city assembly agreed and passed a resolution unanimously favoring his proposal, a "Petition for the General Reconstruction of Hiroshima from the Atomic Bomb Damage." A petition was sent to the government. This developed into a movement to enact a special law initiated by members of the Diet, and the "Hiroshima Peace Memorial City Construction Law" was enacted. Nagasaki City joined the Hiroshima movement and a similar "Nagasaki International Culture City Construction Law" was passed.

In a special poll of residents, carried out on July 7, 1949, an absolute majority approved of the law and it went into effect on August 6, 1949. Under Article 1 of the Hiroshima Peace Memorial City Construction Law which consists of 7 articles, it is written that "This law aims at the construction of Hiroshima as a Peace Memorial City, a symbol of the ideal of making lasting peace a reality."

During the feudal period, Hiroshima prospered as a castle town of the Mōri Clan, one of the influential clans of western Japan, followed by the Fukushima Clan and the Asano Clan. After the Meiji Restoration, it developed and grew into one of the largest and most important military bases of Japan. Destroyed by the first atomic bomb ever used in warfare, Hiroshima rose from the ashes as a Mecca of world peace.

Chapter 2

The Atomic Bomb : Tragedy in Hiroshima

Development of the Atomic Bomb

On December 8, 1941, the Japanese Imperial Army and Navy launched the Pacific War with a surprise attack on Pearl Harbor and a landing in the northern part of the Malay Peninsula. In the initial stages of the war, the Japanese military forces made tremendous advances against the enemy, but after losing the battle of Guadalcanal in 1943, the military situation grew steadily worse.

During this period, the U.S. military forces with utmost secrecy were rushing to develop an atomic bomb, putting a great number of people and great sums of money into this project. Research on the atomic bomb had also been promoted in Japan, in such places as the Tokyo Physico-chemical Research Institute and Kyoto Imperial University. However, no Japanese scientists predicted the completion of an atomic bomb by any country in time for its use in World War II. Totally upsetting this expectation, the U.S. Army finally succeeded in producing and exploding an atomic bomb on July 16, 1945. They erected a steel tower in the desert near Alamogordo in the state of New Mexico, and exploded a nuclear device in its top. The result of the test was astonishingly successful. It was only twenty days later that the atomic bomb was actually dropped on the city of Hiroshima from an airplane on August 6.

Characteristics of Atomic Bombs

The blast force and shock waves from an atomic bomb are destructive over a wide area. However, the fundamental difference between an atomic bomb and a conventional bomb is that the former emits the largest part of its energy in the form of light and heat at the time of explosion, and these thermal rays are able to cause burns or fires even at a relatively long distance from the hypocenter. In addition, an atomic bomb emits a large amount of radiation at the time of explosion which is harmful, invisible, and very strong in its penetrating power. Besides this, the materials exposed to this radiation remain radioactive for a long period of time and are harmful to the human body. These are called "residual nuclear radioactive rays" or "residual radioactivity." Many people who entered the ruined city immediately after the explosion to search for their families or as members of rescue squad suffered the same symptoms as those directly exposed to the atomic bomb explosion.

The Bombs Used on Hiroshima and Nagasaki

In December 1960, in observance of the nineteenth year after the outbreak of the Pacific War, the U.S. Department of Defense and the U.S. Atomic Energy Commission made public pictures and brief descriptions of the atomic bombs which were used on Hiroshima and Nagasaki.

The atomic bomb used for the attack on Hiroshima was referred to by the secret code "Little Boy." The following are its principal characteristics:

1) Hiroshima-type (uranium bomb)
   Length: 120 inches (about 3 meters)
   Diameter: 28 inches (about 0.7 meter)
   Weight: 9,000 pounds (about 4 tons)
   Method of Explosion: Gun-type
   The explosion was caused by the collision of two parts of critical amounts of uranium compacted in a long-shaped bomb.

Hiroshima-type Bomb

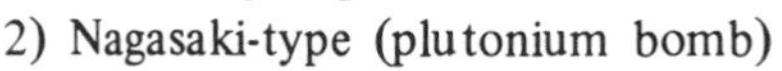

2) Nagasaki-type (plutonium bomb)
   Length: 128 inches (about 3.25 meters)
   Diameter: 60 inches (about 1.5 meters)
   Weight: 10,000 pounds (about 4.5 tons)
   Method of Explosion:
   An explosion of gun powder brought the necessary elements together to trigger the explosion. This bomb was called "Fat Man" and was the bomb used in the New Mexico test.

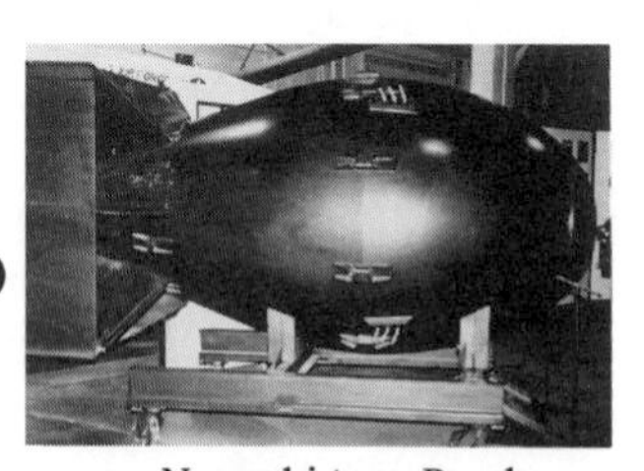

Nagasaki-type Bomb

The Reason for the Dropping of the Atomic Bombs

The energy released in the explosions in both Hiroshima and Nagasaki was thought to be the equivalent of 20 kilotons of conventional high explosive trinitrotoluence (TNT). However, it has been recently estimated to have been 15 kilotons in Hiroshima and 22±2 kilotons in Nagasaki. They were both the first super powerful bombs ever used. For the U.S. forces, since Hiroshima was the first target city for a mid-air explosion after a drop from a plane, it was a very daring operation which required hard training and special prudence. Why was the atomic bomb dropped? Why did Hiroshima become its target?

In his book *Now It Can Be Told,* Major General Leslie R. Groves wrote that the bombing was to be carried out as soon after about August 3 as possible, when weather conditions would assure maximum visibility. Kokura, Hiroshima, Niigata, and Kyoto were considered as possible targets, but after further investigation Hiroshima was chosen as the first target with Kokura and Nagasaki as second and third choices. The bomb was to be dropped as close to the army headquarters in Hiroshima as possible. According to General Groves Hiroshima was chosen because of its military importance. There were 25,000 troops stationed in the city area and Hiroshima was a strategic transportation link between Honshū and Kyūshū. Also, except for Kyoto, it was the largest city in Japan which had not yet suffered extensive damage from air raids. With a population of over 300,000 it was a beehive of small and medium-sized factories manufacturing military supplies. Groves emphasized that Hiroshima was chosen only after careful study. At the same time he recognized that it was only natural that the Japanese people should wonder later why it had been necessary to drop the bomb when Japan was already on the brink of surrender. As reasons for the use of the bomb, General Groves listed, (1) the desire to terminate the war as quickly as possible without the enormous losses in American lives that an invasion of Japan would have entailed, and (2) the desire to handle the occupation of Japan and to direct postwar Japanese affairs without Soviet interference by taking sole credit for the Japanese surrender.

テニアン島を飛び立ち、広島に原子爆弾を投下した
B−29「エノーラ・ゲイ」

The B-29 "Enola Gay"

The Bombing

The B-29, "Enola Gay", carrying the atomic bomb, flew from the U.S. Air Force base on Tinian Island in the Marianas, in the western Pacific. Tinian is 1,700 miles (2,740 kilometers) away from Hiroshima. On July 23, 1944, following the defeat of the Japanese forces, U.S. forces occupied the island. Immediately after that, the U.S. built an air force base which served as a foothold for the attack on the mainland of Japan.

The atomic bomb was carried by a heavy cruiser, the Indianapolis, from San Francisco to the Tinian base. In the early evening of August 5, it was loaded on the Enola Gay, ready to depart at any time.

One of the twelve-man crew of the Enola Gay, Naval Captain William D. Parsons was copilot in charge of installing the atomic bomb. In his flight diary, the times for departure, dropping of the bomb and returning are recorded as follows:

Atomic cloud (photo from one of the three B29s which participated in the raid. Taken about one hour after the bombing from a point 80 kilometers from Hiroshima over the Seto Inland Sea.)

August 6, 1945

2:45 a.m. .... Take off

3:00 a.m. .... Start installing the final triggering device

3:15 a.m. .... Finish installing the triggering device

6:05 a.m. .... Flying over Iwojima to Japan

7:30 a.m. .... Insert the red plug (placing the bomb in position ready to be exploded when dropped)

7:41 a.m. .... Start climbing. Receive information on weather conditions – fair over the 1st and 3rd targets but not over the 2nd

Automatic wireless apparatus transmitting data of explosion (photo courtesy of the Hiroshima Peace Memorial Museum)

8:38 a.m. .... Change to a horizontal flight at an altitude of 32,700 feet (about 9,970 meters)

8:47 a.m. .... Test electronic fuses. Result OK

9:04 a.m. .... Change course toward west

9:09 a.m. .... The target, Hiroshima, in sight

9:15 30" a.m. ... Drop A-bomb

(This is Tinian time. There is an hour's difference between Tinian and Japan, therefore it was 8:15 in Hiroshima.)

As soon as the atomic bomb was released at an altitude of 31,600 feet (about 9,600 meters), the Enola Gay made a quick turn of 158 degrees to the north with the bomb under visual observation. It fled away toward the skies of the Sanin district. At the same moment an accompanying plane dropped four observation parachutes to confirm the explosion of the atomic bomb. One of the parachutes, picked up later, is on display at the A-bomb Memorial Museum.

Confirmation In the evening of the day the U.S. dropped the atomic bomb on Hiroshima, shortly after midnight on the seventh in Japan, President Truman made a radio announcement to the world: "Sixteen hours ago an American airplane dropped one bomb on Hiroshima, Japan, and destroyed its usefulness to the enemy. That bomb had more power than 20,000 tons of T.N.T. It had more than two thousand times the blast power of the British Grand Slam, which is the largest bomb ever yet used in the history of warfare. .... It was an atomic bomb." The Japanese government heard the announcement, but the army insisted that it was U.S. strategic propaganda and until an actual survey in Hiroshima proved that it was really an atomic bomb, no steps were to be taken. Since the Japanese government was afraid that this incident would cause unwillingness among the Japanese people to fight the war on the mainland of Japan, it treated the incident very lightly.

After a series of discussions, the government with great pressure from the military authorities, released the following statement.

The Imperial Headquarters announced at 15:30 on August 7, 1945:

1. On August 6, Hiroshima was attacked by a B-29 aircraft resulting in tremendous damage.
2. The enemy seems to have used a new type of bomb to attack Hiroshima, but the details are now under investigation.

Despite the fact that a second bomb was dropped on Nagasaki on the ninth, and the survey team reported that it was an atomic bomb that had been dropped on Hiroshima, the military authorities did not inform the Japanese people of the truth – that atomic bombs had been used – until the fifteenth, the end of the war.

August 6 As the U.S. Air Force repeated air-raids over all of Japan, its cities one after another were turned into wide stretches of burnt ruins. Hiroshima alone had long been spared. As August came, no plane came into sight on the second and the third, but on the evening of the fifth, the air-raid sirens sounded again and again. Each time, defense personnel took up their appointed positions, old people and women went back and forth to the air-raid shelters and there was hardly any time for sleep.

At 0:25 a.m. on the sixth, the air-raid warning was sounded again, but at 2:10 the all clear was sounded, and 5 minutes later the alert was also withdrawn. At 7:09 a.m. the radio announced that four B-29s were in the skies northwest of Hiroshima, but they soon left. At 7:31 a.m. it was reported "no enemy planes are in sight in the military jurisdiction of Chūgoku district." One of those enemy planes, scouting the weather of Hiroshima City, reported that the weather being clear, it was possible to proceed with the bombing. Of course the people of the city had no means of knowing this. When the "all-clear" was announced, the citizens, freed from the strain which had lasted from the previous night, gave a sigh of relief, since air-raids were almost always carried out at night.

Dismantling of Buildings

On that morning, work was in progress on the sixth stage of dismantling buildings in order to make fire breaks as protection from air-raids. The national volunteer corps from various districts and industries and mobilized students in the lower grades of middle schools and girls' schools, under orders to start their work at seven o'clock, gathered at the appointed places one after another. Volunteer corps (about 10,000 people) from neighboring towns and villages had entered the city to join them.

Figures for the number of buildings dismantled and people evacuated follow:

	Buildings	People	the aged, infants, and pregnant women
the first stage (at the end of 1944)	400 households	1,029 cases (4,210 persons)	
the second stage (from Feb. to March, 1945)	2,454 households	5,532 cases (21,710 persons)	6,561 households (25,920 persons)
the third stage (in April, 1945)		1,550 households	
the fourth stage (in May, 1945)		2,380 households	
the fifth stage (from June to July, 1945)		4,000 households	
the sixth stage (from July to Aug., 1945)		6,000 households (2,500 completed)	

(quated from the *New Edition of The Police History of Hiroshima Prefecture*)

During work on the sixth stage, the A-bomb was dropped. The sites for this demolition work were: (1) around Zakoba-chō (behind the present City Hall) (2) around Dobashi (Koami-chō, Nishi-shin-machi, Sakai-machi) (3) around the Prefectural Office (Kako-machi, Tenjin-chō, Naka-jima-shin-machi, Zaimoku-chō) (4) around the Tsurumi Bridge, and the Hijiyama Bridge (Tsurumi-chō, Shōwa-machi) (5) around the Telegraph Corps (Minami-machi) (6) around Hatchōbori.

The skies of Hiroshima were perfectly clear, a beautiful bluish purple, without a speck of cloud. The scorching sun of midsummer poured down on the city, and those in the demolition work were dripping with sweat.

The Explosion of the Atomic Bomb

The air-raid warning was issued from the strategy room in the semi-basement of the Chūgoku District Military Headquarters in Hiroshima Castle. Employees of the Hiroshima Central Broadcasting Station were always on duty there to be in communication with the main station, then located in Kami-Nagarekawa-chō. The news was released to the citizens by radio from there.

Shortly after eight, an order to issue an air-raid warning came in and the bell rang. Masanobu Furuta, the announcer on duty, immediately rushed into the office. And then hurrying down the hallway, he looked over the news manuscript which read, "8:13 a.m. Chūgoku District Army Announcement: Three large enemy planes proceeding westward over Saijō area. Strict precautions should be taken." As soon as he got into the studio, he pushed the buzzer. It was 8:15 a.m.

He began to read over the air, "Chūgoku District Army Announcement: Three large enemy planes proceeding over Saijō area .... ", there was a tremendous noise. He felt the reinforced concrete building tilt, and his body seemed to float in the air. The attack hit the citizens of Hiroshima without warning.

As a brilliant thermal flash covered the city with a tremendous roaring blast, Hiroshima was instantly leveled to the ground. A huge pillar of flame shot up into the air and volumes of smoke curled into the sky.

The whole city turned into an inferno with the dead and wounded lying everywhere. Many parts of the city caught fire and soon the conflagration had spread all over the city. In the midst of the flames and the raging whirlwind, crowds of people either naked or half-naked, covered with blood all over their bodies, fled from the scene and died one after another. Countless people were burnt to death, caught under the collapsed buildings and other materials. People calling out for their close relatives and asking for help were heard through the terrible blaze. Almost all died in the flames. Although the explosion occurred just as the tide was beginning to ebb, the rivers which flow through the city were full of dead bodies and scraps of buildings which had been blown there by the blast. A large number of people escaped to the river banks only to sink in the water out of sheer exhaustion.

The Power of the Bomb According to the reports made by various university research groups, the atomic bomb was exploded in the air about 600 meters above the city. The hypocenter was said to be approximately 125 meters south of the eastern entrance to the baseball stadium (at that time the site of a Torii of the Gokoku Shrine) which is located along the Kamiya-chō streetcar lines, about 25 meters southeast of the front entrance of the Shima surgical hospital (formerly, 19, Saiku-machi).

As the bomb was exploded, a fireball 100 meters in diameter (60 meters, according to another account) was formed in the air. Its temperature, 1/10,000 second after the explosion, reached approximately 300,000 degrees Celsius within a 17-meter radius and to 9,000 to 11,000 degrees within a radius of 50 meters. It is estimated that at a point directly beneath the hypocenter the heat was at least 6,000 degrees.

According to the report of the U.S. army observation plane, 5 minutes after the explosion, the mushroom cloud caused by the explosion, hung as a mammoth cloud of dark-gray color about 3 miles in diameter (approximately 5 kilometers) over the center of the city. From the center of the cloud a pillar of white smoke rose, reaching to an altitude of 35,000 feet (about 17,000 meters) and spreading out at the top. Four hours after the bombing, a photo-reconnaissance plane flew over Hiroshima. At that time the whole city was still covered by a cloud of smoke so thick that people in the plane could see flames only at the edges of the city.

The destructive power of the atomic bomb with the composite effect of the blast and the thermal rays was utterly beyond imagination. Let us summarize the record of the *Atomic Bomb Damage Survey Report* issued by the Science Council of Japan.

It is estimated that the intensity of the pressure right under the hypocenter was about 4.5 to 6.7 tons per square meter for a duration of about 0.4 seconds.

Within a 2-kilometer radius of the hypocenter, all wooden buildings were leveled and burnt to ashes. Most of the concrete buildings were not flattened, but all their windows were blown out and their interiors were completely devastated by fire. It is thought that within a 1.8-kilometer radius the fires were started by the direct rays of the radiant heat,

Ruins in Hon-dōri (Photo by Shigeo Hayashi)

though there were some houses that were burnt by the embers from cooking fires. Also the wooden houses standing within a 2- to 4-kilometer radius of the blast were totally or partially destroyed depending on the distance from the blast. But fires did not break out except in rare cases such as the Zuisen Temple, located in Onaga-chō, 2.7 kilometers from the hypocenter, which was burnt to the ground when the radiant heat ignited the straw-thatched roof of the temple. The fires began to spread at around 9 o'clock in the morning and burned most furiously from 10 o'clock to 2 o'clock in the afternoon. The violent fire consumed everything, though the flames began to weaken before darkness came. In some places the flames were still rising for several days.

Windows were blown out over a very wide area. One of the buildings of the Mitaki Temple in Mitaki-chō, about 3.2 kilometers from the hypocenter, was partially destroyed, its roof tiles were blown off, and its windows were smashed to pieces. The bomb blast was felt even at a distance of 60 kilometers. In Miyoshi City situated 62 kilometers northeast of Hiroshima City, people could see the flash of the bomb, hear the sound of the explosion, and feel a slight concussion. There were some people who felt the bomb blast on the Tomoe Bridge there. The destructive power of the bomb was so strong that people who were quite a distance from the city were injured by flying pieces of glass.

Throughout the day of August 6, 1945, a monstrous tower-shaped cumulonimbus cloud hung over the city. For 20 or 30 minutes after the explosion, the black cloud moved north-north west (in the direction of former Asa County). From 9 o'clock in the morning to about 4 o'clock in the afternoon it brought rain showers. The showers were not heavy in the center of the city; however, in the north (Kabe area) and in the west (Koi and Takasu areas), there were torrential rains. In some districts the rainfall reached 50 to 100 millimeters over a period of 1 to 3 hours. This helped to extinguish the forest fires in Koi and the surrounding mountain areas.

In the beginning the rain came in large, muddy, sticky, pitch-black drops, coarse enough to give pain to the naked bombing victims. The "black rain" lasted for 1 or 2 hours and was then followed by normal rain.

The black rain contained the muddy dust which was produced at the time of the explosion and went up in black smoke, and soot from the resulting fires. Also, it contained radioactive substances from the bomb, which were floating in the air or had fallen to the ground. In the midst of the rain the temperature suddenly fell so that people wearing nothing or only light clothes, who escaped from the fire, shivered with cold even though it was a hot day in midsummer.

Since this rain contained strong radioactivity, people who were exposed to it showed the same symptoms as those who were directly hit by the explosion of the atomic bomb. Also fish, such as carp in ponds and catfish and eel in rivers, died and floated up to the surface of the water, because the radioactive-contaminated rainwater fell into these ponds and rivers. The cattle that ate the grass wet by the muddy rain developed diarrhea. Many people also suffered from the same symptoms, for the city water pipes were broken and they had to drink well water (underground water).

Deaths and Casualties Followed One After Another

There was no time either to feel the flash, or to hear the sound of the explosion for the people within a radius of about 500 meters of the hypocenter. This area was completely destroyed and burnt to ashes by the direct hit of the A-bomb. After the fire only a pile of white ashes remained. People who were within a radius of about 1,000 to 2,000 meters were burnt by the thermal flash, or injured by the fragments of glass and other materials. A number of people were blown away by the blast wind and lost consciousness. It all happened in an instant. A quiet summer morning, all of a sudden, turned into a terrible hell.

Throngs of bloodstained people, naked or half-naked, were dragging themselves along, trying to find safety. There were countless dead. There were the wounded, sitting dazed or crying for help. However, no one had enough energy to spare for helping someone else. It was all they could do to drag themselves forward one step at a time.

Exodus to the Suburbs

Those who were not killed immediately who lived in the eastern part of the city, escaped temporarily either to Hijiyama Park, the Sen Estate (presently named Shukkeien), the Eastern Drill Ground (north of Hiroshima Station and the area at the foot of Mt. Futaba), or the Niho and Ōkō areas (around Mt. Ōgon). From there, as they were able, they fled into Aki County toward Kaitaichi Station, toward Fuchū, or toward the Fudōin in Ushita. Others went up the river from Hakushima toward Hesaka Village.

Akatsuki unit Ujina camp

People living in the northern part of the city made their escape to the vicinity of Kabe town in Asa County through Yokogawa and Ōshiba Park. Those who were able went on to various places in the same county. There were quite a few people who hid themselves in the neighboring Mitaki Temple or in the mountains near Nagatsuka.

People living in the western part of the city escaped either to the airfield in Yoshijima-chō, or to the athletic field in Minami-Kannon-machi, or to the firing range and Mitsubishi Heavy Industries plants in Eba-chō. Later they escaped across the river toward Koi, Takasu or Furue, using the remaining bridge or by boats and rafts which long before had been prepared for an emergency. Some went farther to various places in Saeki County, such as Itsukaichi and Hatsukaichi. There were also many people who took shelter in the nearby mountains.

Most people living to the south of Hiroshima City Hall went to the Miyuki Bridge. From there they fled toward Ujina where there were no fires. Among them were a number of people who lived in the islands located in the Seto Inland Sea. Ujina Port was in great turmoil all through the day as these people tried to find transportation back to their homes. More than ten thousand wounded were carried by boat to such islands as Ninoshima, Kanawajima, Etajima, and Nōmijima. Strangely enough, some people fled by mistake into the burning area near the hypocenter where they were trapped and burned to death.

The number of people who escaped to Aki, Asa, and Saeki Counties, and other places reached 150,000, including the wounded sent by train, and by trucks of the Akatsuki Unit from Ujina. Apart from those who were transported by train and truck, most of the hibakusha made their way as best they could on foot. Many fell dead on the way.

Public and private hospitals in the vicinity of the city, including the Teishin Hospital (supported by the Ministry of Communications) in Hakushima-chō, which was virtually wrecked by the bomb blast, the Red-Cross Hospital in Senda-machi, the Army Mutual Aid Hospital and the barracks for ship-training corps in Ujina-chō, the branch of the Army Hospital in Eba-chō, the Mitsubishi Hospitals (affiliated with Mitsubishi Heavy Industries Corporation) in Kannon-machi and Eba-chō, and other hospitals were crowded with the wounded who filled the buildings and overflowed into the yards of these buildings. However, only a few doctors and nurses were able to work, for most had been either killed or seriously wounded. In addition, medical supplies were almost instantly exhausted and further supplies were unavailable. During the night treatment continued in the darkness. A woman doctor, recalling the situation later said, "The treatment I could give to the wounded was only to apply mercurochrome or ointment. But soon these ran out too. I could do nothing but give water to those who called for it as they approached death."

Relief Activities Immediately After the Explosion

An army shipping unit (commonly known as the Akatsuki Corps stationed at Ujina, was damaged only slightly by the A-bomb, since Ujina was 4 kilometers away from the hypocenter. The corps immediately informed the Naval Base at Kure of the disastrous situation in Hiroshima and at the same time, sent relief teams to the city. The relief teams went into the central part of the city, which was engulfed in flames. Some of the teams went by land, and others used the Ōta River.

All of the reverbanks in the city were covered with hibakusha seeking refuge from the flames. Almost all of them were severely injured and dying. The sight was a living hell. The relief units who came overland had great difficulty because of the fire. They managed to arrive at the badly damaged main office of the street-car company at Senda-machi around noon. There, they had to spend nearly the whole afternoon waiting for the fire to die down. As they encountered hibakusha on their way to the central part of the city, they sent them to places of safety in Ujina (Army Barracks etc.) and to school buildings in the suburbs, using trucks and boats. At this time, a large number of hibakusha were sent to Ninoshima Island.

In the early evening of the day of the explosion, a temporary office of the Hiroshima Prefectural Government was set up in the severely-damaged Tamon-in Temple in Hijiyama Park. A call for help was issued from this temporary office to the neighbouring local governments and police stations as well as to the Central Government. In order to ask for help, they had to walk to undamaged public facilities in the suburbs to place the telephone calls.

The following day, a joint meeting of representatives of the military, government and private sector was held in the air-raid shelter of Futabayama under the direction of the Second High Command of the Military, and a countermeasures committee was formed. The counter-measures committee issued rescue requests to military bases and universities nearby.

Because of these emergency rescue requests, medical teams, voluntary guards, and other groups for relief activities were organized in the neighbouring cities and towns. Those medical teams and volunteers came to

Hiroshima with their own food and other relief items and started rescue activities at various points in the city without taking any rest. However, the number of the victims was so huge that they soon ran short of medical supplies, and large numbers of hibakusha died without receiving any medical treatment.

At the Termination of the War

The end of the war finally came on August 15 amidst great confusion. Where the city of Hiroshima had once been there was only a great emptiness. It was about a month after the holocaust before calmness gradually came back; doctors and medical supplies were somehow procured, and medical activities became somewhat normal. Even so, there were some seriously wounded hibakusha, who committed suicide because of their frightful scars or great pain. Many lost their entire families and all their friends at one stroke and fell into complete loneliness. Furthermore, the violent flood damage caused by the Makurazaki typhoon which started around midnight of September 17, left people in complete hopelessness. As a result of this total despair, some were driven to insanity. The flood waters finally extinguished the pale phosphorus flames which had still been visible every night in the burnt-out area and washed away the stench of the dead bodies. Only a few figures were to be seen in the vast expanse of the ruined city and no sound was to be heard. The reality of defeat in war was pressed home to those few survivors eking out their meager existence.

Surveys of Atomic Bomb Casualities

Immediately after the bombing, the Akatsuki Corps and the Kure Naval Base dispatched rescue teams to rescue the wounded, to dispose of corpses and to clear off the main streets. They also sent survey teams to determine the actual damage caused by the bomb and to take measures for defense and for medical treatment for the injured.

At the same time, the Imperial Headquarters dispatched a survey team to determine whether the bomb dropped on Hiroshima was an atomic bomb or not. In addition to these survey teams, a team was dispatched by the Technology Agency. The details are recorded in the *Record of the Hiroshima A-bomb War Disaster* (vol. I) published by Hiroshima City. According to the record, on the evening of August 10, a joint Army-Navy meeting was held at the Hiroshima Army Ammunition Dump with the presence of Dr. Nishina and Dr. Arakatsu of the Army and Navy survey teams, and officers of the Second High Command, the Akatsuki Corps and the Kure Naval Station. Each survey team reported its findings. They compiled the "Hiroshima Bombing Survey Report" and reported to the Imperial Headquarters in Tōkyo that the bomb was an A-bomb. The surveys were conducted rather hurriedly under war-time conditions. Systematic and scientific surveys by authorities in various fields were first conducted after the war ended. The survey treatment team led by Dr. Masao Tsuzuki of Tokyo University arrived in Hiroshima and announced their treatment plans for hibakusha on August 30. Until that time, neither physicians nor A-bomb survivors knew any way of treating radiation disease.

Later various universities sent survey teams to Hiroshima. On September 8, for the first time the U.S. Occupation Forces dispatched a survey team led by Thomas Farrel. Dr. Marcel Junod, Chief Representative to Japan of the International Red Cross Committee, accompanied this team. They determined the levels of residual radioactivity and carried out a preliminary study on the effects of the A-bomb.

On September 14, the Ministry of Education established the Special Committee for the Investigation of A-bomb Damage, headed by Dr. Haruo Hayashi, chairman of the Scientific Research Council of Japan. This Special Committee had nine sections. It continued the survey in Hiroshima and Nagasaki until March, 1946. Some sections conducted surveys for 3 years until 1947. In August, 1951, the Special Committee published the *Atomic Bomb Casualty Investigation Report* (summary report) and two volumes of the full report in May, 1953. The documentary film crew of the Nippon Eiga-sha (Japan Film Corporation) accompanied the scientists of the Special Committee and participated in the documentation of A-bomb damage. They produced invaluable films in various fields. There are also many photographs taken by military cameramen and private citizens. They have become very important A-bomb materials.

At the same time, the U.S. Military was anxious to ascertain the power of an A-bomb dropped on a city in actual warfare, rather than in a test in a deserted area. The Japan-U.S. Joint Commission was formed by the GHQ Army Surgeons Team headed by A. W. Oughterson – GHQ Consultant Surgeon, the Manhattan Engineer District Investigation Group headed by Thomas Farrel, and Dr. Masao Tsuzuki and other Japanese scientists who were requested to join the survey by the U.S. Army survey teams. The Hiroshima group of the Joint Commission entered Hiroshima on October 12 and conducted a comprehensive survey on the effects of the A-bomb. Most of the materials including photographs that the Japanese team had collected were then taken back to the U.S. A U.S. Strategic

Bombing Survey was also conducted. Most of the survey materials were later returned to Japan or donated to Hiroshima University as well as to the Hiroshima Peace Culture Foundation and the A-bomb Memorial Museum, where the materials have been widely used.

The Number of Hibakusha

In prewar days the population of Hiroshima City under normal conditions had been approximately 440,000. However, as residents were evacuated and buildings dismantled in preparation for air raids, the population decreased significantly. The population at the time of the explosion was 312,277 according to a survey published on August 10, 1946, by the Research Section of the Hiroshima City Hall. In addition to this, about 40,000 soldiers were probably stationed in the city. So the total figures of the settled population at that time would be about 350,000. However, the day-time population would have been significantly larger because evacuees living in suburban towns and villages entered the city for work at various government offices, companies and factories each day. Also about 20,000 people from neighboring villages were mobilized for demolition of buildings and houses. (This figure is based on "*A New History of Hiroshima City.*) Adding these figures to the resident population, some 370,000 people were in the city at the crucial moment, although some estimate the number at about 400,000 because of the sharp increase in the daytime population.

It is extremely difficult to determine the actual number of hibakusha, since the population of that day itself remains unclear. Only estimated figures are known even today. So far, a variety of statistics concerning human casualties have been released. The following are important ones.

* Figures released by the Hiroshima Police Headquarters on November 30, 1945.

Dead	78,150	
Seriously wounded	9,428	
Slightly wounded	27,997	
Missing	13,983	(presumed. dead)
Other victims	176,987	
Total	306,545	

* Figures released by the Research Section of Hiroshima City Hall on August 10, 1946.

Dead		118,661
Wounded		79,130
(Breakdown)	Seriously wounded	30,524
	Slightly wounded	48,606

Missing	3,677
Total victims	201,468
Persons without any injury	118,613

In a document addressed to the General Secretary of the United Nations from the mayors of Hiroshima and Nagasaki in November 1976, it is reported that the number of deaths by the end of December 1945, was approximately 140,000 (± 10,000). It is also reported that more than 40,000 military personnel were exposed to the A-bomb, whereas civilians were 310,000 to 320,000. The document also declares that in addition to Japanese many non-Japanese people were also killed by the A-bomb, including Koreans who were brought to Japan for. forced labor during the war, exchange students from China and south Asian countries, and American soldiers who were captured.

Atomic Bomb Disease

People within a radius of approximately 4 kilometers of the blast were seriously affected by the radiation. This included people who were not present at the time of the bombing but experienced the "black rain" which followed. The first part of the body to be affected was the blood. This was followed by disturbances in the blood-producing tissues of the bone marrow, the spleen and the lymph glands. The lymphocytes are especially susceptible to radiation and are destroyed immediately. Later on the internal organs such as the lungs, the stomach and intestines, the liver and kidneys are affected.

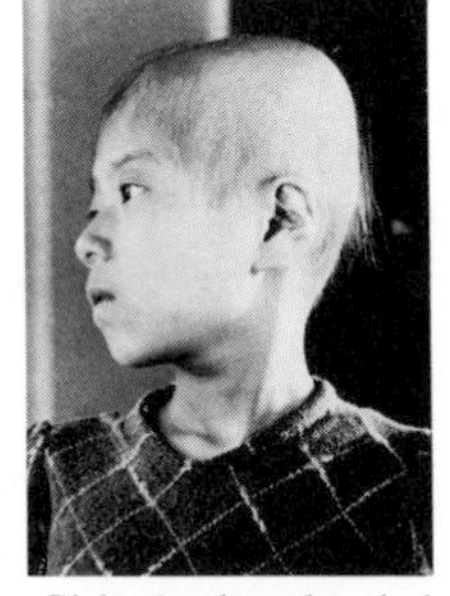

Girl who lost her hair from radiation (exposed in Funairi-chō, 1 kilometer from the hypocenter, began to lose hair two months after the bombing. Photo by Shunkichi Kikuchi)

Most of those who received a high degree of such radioactivity died from within a few days up to two weeks. The majority of those who received a more moderate degree of radioactivity died within two to four weeks after developing severe symptoms. Many specialists, who came to Hiroshima after the dropping of the A-bomb for medical research and investigation, have reported that those who received a lower degree of the radioactivity were easily affected by various illnesses for several months, even though their lives were spared.

Among those who were most seriously affected were those who were out of doors and were struck by the thermal and light waves and the actual bomb blast in addition to the radioactivity. They either died instantly or within a few days. Those who did survive had such serious symptoms as high fever, extreme general malaise, general sense of weakness, emesis, hematemesis, hemoptysis, blood discharge from the bowels and hematuria. They all died within a short period of time.

Many of those who received a moderate degree of radioactivity suffered from emesis immediately after the bombing, and anorexia and complete lack of appetite, lasting for several days. After some period of time hair epilation and hemorrhage were observed in many people.

On the other hand, as described in many records of personal experiences published thus far, many of those who were not heavily exposed to the radiation escaped to the suburbs. They kept up their physical strength with rest, while eating fresh vegetables and fruits. As a result of such efforts, they passed the crisis. However, radiation sickness, heavy or slight, is incurable. Radioactivity is like a bullet which can cause the self-destruction of the human race.

The report of the medical survey commission states, "It is adequate to call the physical disturbances caused by radiation either 'Atomic Bomb Radiation Disease' or 'Atomic Bomb Radiation Damage'." At first many people used the term "Atomic Bomb Damage", but later on the term "Atomic Bomb Disease" became more common.

Hibakusha Relief Measures

There were no official relief measures for the hibakusha taken until January, 1953, when the Hiroshima Medical Association organized the Hiroshima Council for Countermeasures Against A-Bomb Diseases, and started relief activities. This was due to the fact that the strict control by the U.S. over the release of information on the A-bomb and the publication of medical research kept anything from being done for the hibakusha until Japan became free when the Peace Treaty went into effect in 1952. In March, 1954, the Lucky Dragon (Number 5 Fukuryū-maru), which had been operating in an area 80 nautical miles from Bikini Atoll, was showered with radioactive ash resulting from an H-bomb test. The life of a fisherman was lost in the accident. In October the government organized and started the Liaison Council for Investigation of Relief Measures for the A-Bomb Victims, and showed indications of being willing to pass a relief law.

In May, 1956, the cities of Hiroshima and Nagasaki, pressed by citizens' groups, produced the draft of a bill, giving impetus to the movement for the enactment of such a law. This effort resulted in the promulgation of law NO. 41 – "The A-Bomb Medical Law" on March 31, 1957. This law secured health examinations and medical benefits for certified hibakusha. On May 20, 1968, law NO. 53 – "The Hibakusha Special Welfare Law" was promulgated to promote the welfare of hibakusha and the stabilization of their livelihood. A movement to secure the enactment of a Hibakusha Relief Law has been carried on actively; however, little progress has been made.

Chapter 3

The Peace Memorial Park and Its Environs

Before the Dropping of the A-Bomb

Peace Memorial Park

The area, located between the Motoyasu River and the Hon River, presently called the Peace Memorial Park, includes the prewar Tenjin-chō Kita-gumi, Zaimoku-chō, Nakajima-hon-machi and Motoyanagi-chō. This area was the business center of Hiroshima from its days as a castle town until the 1920s. General stores, theaters, restaurants and Japanese inns stood side by side, busy day and night. However, during the 1920s the business center moved to the eastern part of the city (around Hatchō-bori). Only the streets remained as reminders of the area's prosperous past.

There were quite a few historic temples and shrines in this area. In Nakajima-hon-machi there was a temple called Jisenji and the area around Jisenji was generally called Jisenji-no-hana. The Seigan, Denpuku and Jōen temples in Zaimoku-chō and the Tenmangū in Tenjin-chō were especially popular among the citizens. Outisde the Park, the Awashima Daimyōjin (popularly called Awashima-san) in the precincts of the Seifukuin in Kobiki-chō, the Konpira-san on the grounds of the Jimyōin, the Kasamori-san in the precincts of the Myohō Temple in Zaimoku-chō, the Koyasu-Kannon on the ground of the Anrakuin and the Nankō-san in the precincts of the Keizōin were also popularly worshiped by the citizens.

By drawing a map of the area before the dropping of the A-bomb, the Research Institute for Nuclear Medicine and Biology of Hiroshima University and NHK (Japan Broadcasting Corporation) Hiroshima station, made a survey to determine the number of people who were living in the area where the Peace Park is now located. When ninety percent of the survey was completed they reported that there had been 710 shops and houses with 2,611 people. Actually there would have been more people if they had not had to move out for evacuation and other reasons. About 1,000 houses were evacuated before August 6, 1945.

Disaster

This area, the closest to the hypocenter, was instantly annihilated by the atomic bomb. There is no way to know the actual conditions in the area at the time of the explosion because almost no one survived. Only those who were on duty in businesses and factories in the suburbs, or those who were out on private business, escaped the destruction. After the explosion they tried desperately to enter the area; however, flames prevented them from doing so. At about six o'clock in the evening the fire burnt itself out after consuming all the combustible materials. Only in Tenjin-chō, did the fires continue to burn. When people entered the area searching for survivors among the flames, they found a group of girl students lying on the bank of the Motoyasu River, holding one another. These students had been exposed to the A-bomb while working in the area around the prefectural office building (Kako-machi, Nakajima-shin-machi, Tenjin-chō, and Zaimoku-chō) where they had been ordered to assist in demolition work. Most of them had been burnt to death and their faces were completely unrecognizable. A few girls were still breathing faintly but they were dying and there were so many of them that without rescue teams and equipment nothing could be done to save them.

The work of evacuating the dead began the next day (a small amount was done already on August 6). Using the Akatsuki units from Ujina and voluntary guards from neighboring districts, the corpses were gathered together beside bridges or on vacant land where the houses had been demolished, and cremated by igniting gasoline poured over the bodies. The ashes were handed over on the spot if relatives claimed them. The unidentified ashes were stored in one place.

The Burnt-Out City

Autumn came but the city was still a wide stretch of burnt over ruins. Around October, when horseweeds grew thickly, several shacks at last appeared. A few people had started living there again. In December the number of shacks increased, but living conditions were so bad that people were on the verge of starvation.

Around the first anniversary of the A-bomb victims' deaths, white grave posts were set up in various parts of the burnt city. It looked as if the whole city was a graveyard.

Making a Reconstruction Plan

Hiroshima had become a city of death. Its rebuilding would be a difficult task.

The various agencies of government devoted themselves to plans for reconstruction. Already in November 1945, the city assembly organized a reconstruction committee. In December of the same year, the Hiroshima War Damage Reconstruction Committee, made up of block representatives, began to function. In January 1946, the Hiroshima Reconstruction Bureau was set up to carry out various reconstruction measures. Through the efforts of these administrative organs the reconstruction of the city was pushed forward. The municipal authorities, the city assembly, and its citizens worked together to design a modern city plan. The construction of the Peace Boulevard (generally called the 100-meter-wide avenue) and the memorial park (presently called the Peace Park) in Nakajima-chō district was already decided on at this time. There were many opinions expressed, but there was consensus among the people concerned that the new Hiroshima City should become a Peace Culture City. However, carrying out the city's reconstruction plan was very difficult because finances were extremely limited and building supplies were in short supply.

Peace Memorial Projects

In 1947 Shinzō Hamai was elected mayor of Hiroshima in the city's first popular mayoralty election. He declared that the construction of a peace city should be promoted by the Japanese Government and devoted himself to securing the passage of a special law, the "Hiroshima Peace Memorial City Construction Law" ("Peace City Law" for short) which went into effect on August 6, 1949. This law contributed greatly to the later reconstruction of the city both materially and morally.

Peace Memorial Park and other facilities were constructed under this law. As provided by this law, an area of 122,100m^2, including Nakajima Park, and Saiku-machi on the other side of the Motoyasu River (where the Atomic Dome now stands), became the Peace Park. The Peace Memorial Hall, Cenotaph, and other monuments in the Peace Park have become an international mecca for peace.

The site for the Peace Park was secured by the readjustment of city lots requiring landowners to accept substitute lots in other parts of the city. However, since four years had passed since the atomic bombing the area was full of shacks and much difficulty was experienced in getting residents to move elsewhere.

The Gathering of Designs for a New Park

In August 1948, the Hiroshima City Reconstruction Bureau invited the submission of designs for the Peace Memorial Park from all over Japan. The entire Nakajima district was to be made a symbol of lasting peace and a place suitable for recreation and relaxation for all citizens. Its design was to be simple, bringing out the beauty of the environment, and unique, in good, modern taste. A Peace Memorial Tower, Science Memorial Hall, and Cenotaph were to be included in the design. The judges included Mr. Barnes, who was the head of the GHQ religion section; Mr. Jervie, an advisor to Hiroshima City; and Prof. Hideto Kishida of Tokyo University who acted as the head judge. In all there were over 10 judges appointed. By the end of December of that year 145 plans had been submitted, and the joint work of four professors from Tokyo University–Kenzō Tange, Takashi Asada, Yukio Ōtani and Tokukuni Kimura–won first prize. Their drawing included the 100-meter-wide avenue running from east to west on the south of the Peace Park, and Peace Memorial Hall having two separate buildings facing south, the main hall and the meeting hall which were connected by a corridor. In the center of the park was an arch-shaped tower, a peace memorial monument. Green trees were arranged everywhere in the park. From the 100-meter-wide avenue a tourist would be able to see the A-bomb Dome looking through the corridor of the Peace Memorial Hall and through the arch-shaped tower.

Some parts of this construction plan had to be changed before it was actually executed because of the financial predicament of the city and the opinions of the Ministry of Construction. What was to be the main building of the Peace Memorial Hall is now the Peace Memorial Museum (A-bomb Museum) and the corridor has not yet been constructed. The Peace Memorial Hall stands to the east of the museum and the City Auditorium to the west. The plan to build an arch-shaped peace memorial monument was changed to a Memorial Cenotaph in the shape of an ancient Haniwa house. The original plan suggested the planting of low trees in the park so that the entire park would be visible from across the Hon and Motoyasu Rivers. The area to the north of Peace Park where high-rise apartments are built now was planned to be a natural forest park, and a large plaza for the citizens was included in the original blueprint to the south of the castle where Hiroshima Central Library and Hiroshima Art Museum now lie.

Construction of the Peace Park

When construction of the Peace Park was finally to begin, there were about 400 illegal shacks on the site. Responsibility for the clearance of those shacks was shared by the prefectural and the municipal offices. The former took 120 shacks and the latter 280. Clearance work made little progress, partly because many hibakusha (survivors of the atomic bombing) were living in these shacks. As a first step, after acquiring sufficient land for the cenotaph, construction work on that monument was begun. When the ground was leveled for construction, many human bones were exposed, moving the workers to tears.

Introduction of the Peace Memorial Buildings and Monuments

(1) A-bomb Cenotaph

The Construction of the A-bomb Cenotaph (formally called the Memorial Monument for Hiroshima, City of Peace) began in 1951 and on August 6 of the next year, 1952, the unveiling ceremony took place. Stored in it is a register of the names of those who had died in the A-bombing. As of August 6, 1989, 157,071 names are recorded in the 51 volumes of the register. Every year the names of those who have died of A-bomb diseases are reported by their families and friends, and added to the register. The register includes not only the names of Japanese but also those of Koreans and of Americans– Tony —, an ensign of the U.S. Air Force who died in Hiroshima Military Police Headquarters, and John A. Long, an American prisoner who died in the internment camp of the judicial affairs section of the Military Command, Chūgoku District where the Hiroshima Castle once stood.

A-bomb Cenotaph

Since the former arch-shaped cenotaph made of reenforced concrete was heavily damaged after 32 years of its construction, remodeling of the cenotaph started in June, 1984, and the present cenotaph was completed on March 26, 1985. The "Inada Stone", a kind of granite was used in rebuilding the cenotaph. The new cenotaph was constructed in the same size and shape as the original one which Mr. Tange had designed. Placed under the cenotaph are the original stone plate on which the inscription is carved, and the original stone coffin in which the register of the names of those who died of A-bomb diseases is stored. An underground storage for the register was newly built since there will be more names added to the register in the future.

Origin of the Inscription

The A-bomb Cenotaph, in the shape of a clay figure of an ancient house, was designed to keep the souls of those who perished in the atomic bombing out of the rain. Under this arch-shaped cenotaph, there is a black stone coffin in which the register of the names of those who died of A-bomb diseases is placed. The front of the stone coffin reads, "Let All the Souls Here Rest in Peace; For We Shall Not Repeat The Evil."

Inscription

Mayor Hamai commented on the inscription by saying, "Everyone shared the desire to pray for the peace of the dead, however it was difficult to formulate this into a pledge for peace." After racking his brains, Mayor Hamai asked Chimata Fujimoto, his chief secretary, if he had any ideas for an inscription. He thought of his respected teacher, Prof. Tadayoshi Saika of Hiroshima University, an authority on classical inscriptions. Fujimoto visited him immediately in the archery hall where he was living at the time because his residence had been heavily damaged by the bomb. The entrance had a dirt floor and was followed by a low room piled full of books. There was a small desk, but almost no room to move.

Explaining Mayor Hamai's ideas, Fujimoto talked with him for about two hours. The next day Prof. Saika visited Hamai to show him a draft he had written. His draft read, "Rest in Peace; for We Shall Not Repeat The Evil." The words were perfect for expressing what was on his heart. The Mayor decided to adopt Prof. Saika's draft on the spot and asked him to do the handwriting of it which would be engraved on the monument.

When Prof. Saika finished writing, Mayor Hamai could not hide his delight. He took it to the city press club to show it to the reporters. They responded with applause. There was no doubt that the over 200,000 victims were not only the representatives of one nation or one race, but of the whole world, and they should be recognized as a foundation of peace for all human beings. All the people on the earth should make this pledge for a peace without nuclear weapons. However, when the inscription was completed, many people did not understand Mayor Hamai's intention. There were arguments for and against it.

Dr. R.B. Pal, a delegate from India to the World Federation Asian Conference held at Honkawa Elementary School in November, 1952, visited and prayed before the cenotaph. He said in real anger, "It is apparent that "We" in the inscription "For we shall not repeat the evil" means the Japanese people. What is this evil? The cenotaph is dedicated to the souls of the atomic bomb victims. Everyone knows that it was not the Japanese who dropped the atomic bomb. The hands of those who dropped it are not yet cleansed. Even if this evil indicates the previous war, Japan is not responsible for that. That war was a result of the Western powers attempted invasion of the Orient." In the Tokyo War Crimes Trials Dr. Pal maintained to the end that Tōjō and the others were innocent. There were many who expressed agreement with his words.

For an English translation of this inscription, Prof. Saika sent it to his eldest son who was studying at the University of Illinois. He finally settled on the following translation. "Let all the souls here rest in peace; For we shall not repeat the evil." The subject of the sentence is very clear. That is "We" who prostrate ourselves before the cenotaph. All of us who are human beings need to make this pledge. This is a beautiful statement from one who has directly confronted the tragedy of the atomic bomb.

Prof. Saika contributed an article to the city bulletin describing what he meant. "The worst sin committed in the twentieth century is the dropping of the atomic bomb on the city of Hiroshima, but the citizens of Hiroshima are not brooding on the past, but seeking for light toward the future, attempting to do what has not yet been done. It is the privilege of Hiroshima and Nagasaki to resolve that we shall not repeat this evil. If the efforts of Hiroshima brighten the future for all human beings, then the sacrifice made by the victims has not been in vain." From this it is clear that the inscription concerns the past, the present and the future of the human race, not of a particular individual.

(2) Flame of Peace

Behind the cenotaph, at the northern edge of the "Pond of Peace" which was donated by the Japan Junior Chamber of Commerce and Industry on July 31, 1957, there is the "Flame of Peace" which was built with donations from all over Japan. It was designed by Prof. Tange and completed on August 1, 1964. Symbolizing the universal desire for a world free of nuclear weapons, the flame will burn until the day when all such weapons shall have disappeared from the earth. The flame lies in a direct line between the cenotaph and the A-bomb Dome. The pedestal is an abstract rendering of two hands opening upward. At its completion, the flame was lit by representatives of Japanese religious groups and of Japanese industry who brought torches symbolizing region and industry. About 10,000 observers offered silent prayer.

Flame of Peace

(3) Hiroshima Peace Memorial Hall

Its frame work constructed in 1950, the Hiroshima Peace Memorial Hall was finally completed in May, 1955. The aim of the hall is to carry out surveys and do research on various problems related to peace and culture. As a public place appropriate to an international peace culture city, the hall has improved the quality of its permanent displays, and has made efforts to inform the public in the area of peace culture.

Hiroshima Peace Memorial Hall

(4) Hiroshima Peace Memorial Museum

The Hiroshima Peace Memorial Museum is generally called the "A-bomb Museum." Construction was begun in March, 1951, and completed in August, 1955. The building is raised on pillars so that the building itself serves as a magnificent gateway to the park. The architect intended the open area under the building to symbolize the aggressive energy which people should spend working for peace. On the second floor, about 600 atomic bomb materials, picture panels showing scenes of the tragedy, and other related items are displayed. Annual visitors there number more than 1,400,000.

Hiroshima Peace Memorial Museum

Until the A-bomb Museum was built, the "A-bomb Memorial Collection" was set up beside the Hiroshima Central Public Hall which was located next to the Chamber of Commerce and Industry in Moto-machi. Shōgo Nagaoka, who was a part-time civil servant (later he became director of the museum), was in charge of collecting and checking materials related to the bombing. The museum began with these materials. Soon after the bombing, Mayor Hamai forsaw that from an historical point of view all kinds of exposed materials and other related items would have great significance as witnesses to what happened in Hiroshima. He felt very anxious about the future of those materials, fearing that people might carelessly lose them. So he began a policy of collecting such items. That was the beginning of the collection for the museum. In addition to the efforts made by Hamai, the passionate and scholastic devotion given by the director, Nagaoka, and extraordinary cooperation given by many citizens should not be forgotten.

(5) International Conference Center Hiroshima

On July 1, 1989, the International Conference Center Hiroshima opened on the site of the Hiroshima City Auditorium as a key facility for international exchange activities.

The center is filled with various symbols in order to promote international understanding and world peace.

International Conference Center Hiroshima

The center has a grand hall called the Phoenix Hall which will accomodate 1,504 people, as well as 4 conference halls, large and small, which can be used for lectures, meetings and parties.

The center also has a lounge and a library that provides information to local residents and those from abroad.

(6) Fountain of Prayer

In November 1964, the large fountain in front of the A-bomb Museum was constructed by the Hiroshima Bank and donated to the city. The fountain is considered to be the most beautiful in western Japan. Its shape is oval measuring 27 meters from east to west, and 19 meters from north to south. It is divided by a cement wall following the outline of the pool so that there are two ponds, a big one and a small one. It is equipped with 567 spray jets capable of spouting 11 tons of water per minute. It is named "Fountain of Prayer" and dedicated to the souls of those who died in the bombing crying, "Water! Water!" The fountain sends water to a height of 10 meters. At night it is illuminated by 153 underwater lamps in five different colors – red, blue, yellow, green and milky white.

Fountain of Prayer

(7) Children's Peace Monument

The Children's Peace Monument is also called the "Tower of a Thousand Cranes", for many thousands of folded paper cranes are offered there all through the year. The origin of the three-legged monument (tower) can be traced back more than two decades. On the twenty-fifth of October 1955, ten years after the end of the war, a first-year student of Noborimachi Junior High School named Sadako Sasaki died of A-bomb disease in the Hiroshima Red Cross Hospital. Until the end she was hoping for recovery because of a popular belief which says that "folding a thousand paper cranes will bring good luck." The sudden outbreak of her A-bomb disease and her death gave her classmates a great shock. They realized all the more keenly the horror of the A-bomb. Because of this her classmates decided to erect a monument to comfort Sadako's soul and to express their desire for peace. The idea spread and was supported by people all over Japan; this became a large movement so that finally the monument came into being. It was unveiled on Children's Day, May 5, 1958. The designer was an art college professor, Kazuo Kikuchi, and the sponsor was the "Hiroshima Children and Students Association for the Creation of Peace."

Children's Peace Monument

At the top of the 9-meter-high monument there is a bronze statue of a girl stretching her arms up in the air, and holding a golden crane, conveying hope for a peaceful future. Two statues, one on the right and one on the left side of the monument symbolize a boy, a girl, and bright hope.

A bell, modeled after an ancient bronze bell, hangs inside the tower. It was contributed by the Nobel prize winner, Dr. Hideki Yukawa, who was much moved by the feelings of the boys and girls. A golden crane is suspended from the bell so that its sound is like that of a windbell. On the front of the bell "A Thousand Paper Cranes" and on the back "Peace on the Earth and in the Heavens" is inscribed in Dr. Yukawa's handwriting. However, the bell and a golden crane are presently preserved in the Hiroshima Peace Memorial Hall.

Directly under the monument, the words "This is our cry. This is our prayer. For building peace in this world," written by a junior high school student, are carved on a black granite block.

Students from 3,100 schools in Japan and from nine foreign countries contributed to the fund.

(8) A-Bomb Dome

The A-bomb Dome is the ruins of the former Hiroshima Prefecture Industrial Promotion Hall. It is to be preserved as an appeal for world peace and as a witness to the horror of nuclear weapons. The name, A-bomb Dome, grew up among the people of Hiroshima because of the dome-shaped framework left at the top of the central tower.

The background and history of this building:

Around 1912 the decision was made to build a Hiroshima Prefectural Commercial Exhibition Hall in Saiku-machi. It was to be in Secession style, designed and built by the Jan Letzel Construction Company. Jan Letzel was a distinguished Czech architect who designed such buildings as the main building of Sophia University in Tokyo, the Sanyō Hotel in Shimonoseki and the Miyajima Hotel in Itsukushima.

Former Hiroshima Prefecture Industrial Promotion Hall

Construction began in January, 1914, and was completed on April 5, 1915. In the exhibition hall, the products of Hiroshima Prefecture were on permanent exhibition and sold on the spot. After the inauguration of the Hiroshima Prefecture Art Association in 1916, art exhibitions were held every year in this hall. When expositions and country fairs were held at the western drill ground as the main site, the hall was utilized as a second site. So for 30 years after its opening, the hall was widely used by the citizens of Hiroshima. In January 1921 the building's name was changed to the Hiroshima Prefectural Products Exhibition Hall and in November 1933 it became the Hiroshima Prefectural Industrial Promotion Hall.

A-bomb Dome

As the influence of war spread through society, special exhibitions like the Japan-Manchuria Trade Exhibition were held at the hall. As the tide of the war turned sharply against Japan, it was used for various government and semigovernment offices such as the branch office of the Chugoku-Shikoku Public Works, and the Hiroshima District Lumber Corporation. It is said that about 30 people, all those who were inside the hall on the day of the atomic bombing, were killed. The building, located right under the hypocenter, was demolished and burnt out, so that only the framework of the central part of the main building remained.

In July 11, 1966, the Hiroshima city assembly passed a resolution to preserve these ruins, and on April 10, 1967, a ceremony to mark the beginning of the preservation work was held. Mayor Hamai thought that if many people would cooperate in a fund to preserve the building, it would be more meaningful. So he began a nation-wide fund-raising campaign. He himself stood in Sukiyabashi Park in Tokyo collecting funds on the street. This created a great sensation all over Japan. Money was received from individuals and groups not only in Japan but also from the U.S.A., U.S.S.R., France, India and England. The work of reinforcing the building for its preservation was carried out with the cooperation of Hiroshima City, the A-bomb Dome Preservation Technical Committee and the construction company.

At the end of July, 1967, the preservation work was completed and the surroundings were also improved. The desolate triangular park has turned into a place suitable for citizens to come to talk and pray for peace.

(9) Literary Monument Dedicated to Miekichi Suzuki

Literary Monument Dedicated to Miekichi Suzuki

Miekichi Suzuki was a pioneer who raised the quality of Japanese juvenile stories, songs and folktales to the level of "literature." The literary monument in memory of Miekichi Suzuki is located in the greenbelt in front of the A-bomb Dome (east of the Aioi Bridge). The monument stands near the site of his parent's home in what was Sarugaku-chō. It was completed on June 27, 1964, on the 29th anniversary of his death. The monument has two parts. One is a bust of Miekichi placed upon a square granite pillar. On the front of the pillar the words, "Red Bird" are carved in the same style as on the cover of the *Red Bird* which Miekichi edited. Under these words there is a horse's head in relief since Miekichi loved horseback riding. The other part of the monument has bronze figures of a boy and a girl sitting on a granite base in the shape of a book. Miekichi's handwriting is carved on the front of the base: "Like a young boy I will always have dreams. Therefore my anguish will not stay with me long. Miekichi"

This monument was made by Katsuzō Entsuba, a sculptor and a judge for the Nitten Exhibition (the art exhibition sponsored by the Juridical Corporate Association). The Miekichi Suzuki Red Bird Association took the initiative to erect the monument. Miekichi Suzuki died of lung cancer on June 27, 1936, at the age of 54.

(10) Monument to the Old Aioi Bridge

This monument, consisting of the parapet of the former Aioi Bridge and a memorial column, serves as a reminder of the old Aioi Bridge. Originally there were two bridges; one from the former Sarugaku-chō where the monument stands now to Jisenji-no-hana and the other from Jisenji-no-hana to the former Kajiya-chō on the other side of the river. In 1932 the present T-shaped bridge with streetcar lines was built. The name Aioi came from the unique form of the two bridges meeting in Jisenji-no-hana. Jisenji-no-hana, now located on the northern edge of the Peace Park, was then a thriving area with many people coming and going. The expenses for the upkeep of the bridge were met by the tools which pedestrains paid.

Monument to the Old Aioi Bridge

In 1932 the prefectural authorities built a New Aioi Bridge north of the old wooden bridge which decayed and was no longer usable after 1939. In 1940, in order to preserve the achievements of a previous generation, a stone monument was erected where the old bridge from Sarugaku-chō to Jisenji-no-hana had stood. The inscription was hand-written by Nawa Kimoto.

(11) Monument to Those Who Died From the Chūgoku-Shikoku Public Works Office

The monument to those who died from the Chūgoku-Shikoku Public Works Office of the Ministry of Home Affairs (now called Chūgoku-Shikoku District Construction Bureau of the Construction Ministry) is located at the site of the A-bomb Dome. At the time of the explosion, this branch office occupied a room in the Hiroshima Prefecture Industrial Promotion Hall (the A-bomb Dome) and was hit directly by the bomb. The monument, built in memory of the 52 who were killed at work, is made of natural stone, 1.2 meters high and 1.5 meters wide. Standing in the shade of trees beside the dome, the monument has a memorial poem hand-written by Ichirō Abe who was then the head of the office. "Those who were sacrificed to the A-bomb form the foundation for a more peaceful world." The inscription on the back of the monument reads, "While working as volunteers, these 52 employees of the Chūgoku-Shikoku Public Works Office attached to the Ministry of Home Affairs were killed by the A-bomb on August 6, 1945. They rest here, the foundation of a peaceful world. August 6, 1954. The employees of the Chūgoku-Shikoku District Construction Bureau of the Construction Ministry."

Monument to Those Who Died From the Chugoku-Shikoku Public Works Office

These people whose vocation was in "construction" met their deaths as they were involved in "destruction", the demolition of buildings for fire breaks in preparation for bombing raids.

(12) Monument of the Hiroshima District Lumber Control Corporation

This monument, made of a large natural stone and erected on August 6, 1967, stands beside the A-bomb Dome. On the front the words "Rest in Peace" are carved, and on the back "During World War II, the Hiroshima District Lumber Control Corporation, one of the lumber control organs of Japan, had its main office with 260 employees in this building. However, at 8:15 on August 6, 1945, with the explosion of the atomic bomb over one-hundred employees were killed as they went about their duties. When the decision was made to preserve these ruins, the surviving employees gathered at the suggestion of Kōichi Tanaka, who was then the president. This monument is dedicated to our dead fellow-workers, praying for the repose of their souls and for a lasting world peace. It is also dedicated to those who died from the Japan Lumber Corporation, Hiroshima Branch, and the Hiroshima Shipping Lumber Corporation.

Monument of the Hiroshima District Lumber Control Corporation

August 6, 1967. The surviving staff of the Hiroshima District Lumber Control Corporation." The inscription is in the handwriting of Keisen Sone.

(13) Monument to Tamiki Hara

The monument to Tamiki Hara stands in among the trees in front of the A-bomb Dome. The monument was first built at the site of Hiroshima Castle in November, 1951. But due to the damage done to the ceramic plate on which Tamiki's poem was inscribed, it was rebuilt and moved to the present site in 1967.

Monument to Tamiki Hara

A year before poet Tamiki Hara was exposed to the A-bomb while in his parents' house in Nobori-chō, he had lost his beloved wife. The dropping of the A-bomb threw this lonely poet into despair. He committed suicide by throwing himself in front of a train in Tokyo in March, 1951. He was 46 years old. The Japan Pen Club and the Hiroshima Literature Association organized a "Tamiki Hara Committee" and erected this monument to him. The monument was designed by Prof. Yoshirō Taniguchi of Tokyo Technical University. Ceramist, Tōkurō Katō inscribed Tamiki's poem on a ceramic plate, which is set in the front of the monument. The poem reads:

Engraved in stone long ago,
Lost in the shifting sand,
In the midst of a crumbling world,
The vision of one flower.

On the back the words by Haruo Satō, dedicated to the memory of Tamiki Hara, are engraved on a bronze plate. Those who visit this monument are moved by this grief-stricken poet who experienced the death of his wife and then lost the ability to trust human beings because of the dropping of the A-bomb.

When the monument was moved to its present site, black granite was used for the name plate.

(14) Memorial Tower To the Mobilized Students

This tower was erected by the Assocation for the Mobilized Student Victims of Hiroshima Prefecture in May 1967, in the park area to the south of the A-bomb Dome. During the Pacific War, students were mobilized for labor services to increase production and for the demolition of buildings. Among them some 6,000 were killed in the atomic bombing. The tower was built to console the souls of these victims. The twelve-meter high five-story tower, widened toward the top, is finished with Arita-yaki ceramic plates. The Goddess of Peace and eight doves are arranged around it. The center pole of the tower has lights dedicated to the dead. On each side of the tower there are two plaques, each two-meters high showing (1) work to increase food production, (2) girl students sewing, (3) factory work, and (4) lanterns floating in the river. A central plaque gives the historical background of the tower.

Memorial Tower to the Mobilized Students

In August 1944, a student mobilization order was issued, mobilizing students of middle school-age and above for work in military industries. In November of the same year, the Ministry of Home Affairs ordered the construction of fire prevention roads and unoccupied lots for the prevention of fire spreading from air raids. For that purpose about 8,387 students in the advanced course of national elementary schools, middle schools, and girls' high schools in Hiroshima City were mobilized and were in the city when the A-bomb was dropped. Approximately 6,000 students among them died in the bombing. There were also many students who were put in labor services in various industries who died in the atomic bombing.

Their name tablets are laid in state in a box inside the tower. The names of the 372 schools from all over Japan in which the war-dead students were registered are engraved on a copperplate at the rear of the tower.

(15) Atomic Bomb Memorial Mound

The Atomic Bomb Memorial Mound is located at the northwestern end of the Peace Memorial Park. This mound, modeled after an imperial mausoleum of the Momoyama Era, has a small monument on its top. Inside the mound are placed the ashes of tens of thousands of victims of the A-bombing. Most of these are unidentified. When identified, they are handed over to relatives. Immediately after the bombing, countless dead bodies were carried here since the area where the mound is located at present was the center of the bombing. Those dead bodies were cremated by rescue squads and the ashes were gathered together here.

Atomic Bomb Memorial Mound

In January, 1946, an interreligious group, the Society for the Praying for the War Dead, was organized. A temporary memorial mound was built in May, and a temporary vault and chapel in July with money contributed by citizens. In July, 1955, on the occasion of the tenth anniversary of the bombing, a new vault was completed at municipal expense, and the ashes which had been kept in various places were placed there. On August 6, every year, a memorial service is offered by the people of Hiroshima with the help of the Hiroshima Religious Federation.

(16) Monument of Prayer

The Monument of Prayer is situated to the right behind the A-bomb Cenotaph. It was built on August 15, 1960, on the fifteenth anniversary of the end of the war, by the Committee to Carry out a National Festival of Prayers for Peace to Comfort the Spirits of the Dead, sponsored by the New Japan Association. This monument is dedicated to peace and to the comfort of those who died for their country in various crises including the Greater East Asia War. The monument has the figures of a young couple on a pedestal holding their child in their arms. It was sculptured by Yoshizumi Yokoe, who is on the board of trustees of Nitten (the art exhibition sponsored by the Juridical Corporate Association). As one steps on a stone placed in front

Monument of Prayer

of the pedestal, a music box plays "Spirits, do not weep beneath the ground" from inside the pedestal. To the right facing the monument there is a stone with a poem of Atsuo Ōki, a poet born in Hiroshima, titled "Praying for the peaceful rest of the departed souls and for peace."

(17) Figure of the Merciful Goddess of Peace (Kannon)

Figure of the Merciful Goddess of Peace (Kannon)

This figure is in what was formerly Nakajima-hon-machi, a busy business area. It was burnt to the ground and most of its residents were killed by the A-bomb. After the war, the Peace Park included this area. Surviving residents gathered and formed the Nakajima-hon-machi Association. They erected this figure on August 6, 1956, as an expression of their regret at parting with their old community which had ceased to exist, and as a prayer for the repose of the deceased. On the front of the pedestal, "the Merciful Goddess for Peace" is carved, on the back "Oh, the site of Nakajima-hon-machi! August 6, 1956 Tadao Watanabe, Mayor of Hiroshima." In front of this figure there is a map of Nakajima-hon-machi before the A-bombing, which was made by its former residents. The names of those who lived in Nakajima-hon-machi and died in the A-bombing are inscribed on the stone tablet beside the figure.

(18) Peace Bell

Peace Bell

The ceremony for the first striking of the Peace Bell took place on September 20, 1946, upon completion of the bell. A world map with no national boundaries symbolizing "One World" is engraved on the surface of the bell which is 1.5-meters long and 1,200 kilograms in weight. This is the work of Masahiko Katori who is known as a master bell-maker. The wooden bell hammer was made from a 90-year-old pine tree contributed by Yachiyo-chō, Takata County, Hiroshima Prefecture. The concrete belfry in the shape of a dome, expressing the universe, with four pillars supporting the roof, is surrounded by a pond, 2-meter wide and 80-centimeter deep, in which the "Ōga" lotus, a yellow flowering lotus donated by the Crown Prince, is planted.

This bell was built with offerings from all over Hiroshima Prefecture collected by a group led by Kengyō Nishimura, a Buddhist scholar. Visitors are encouraged to toll the bell freely.

(19) Peace Clock Tower The Peace Clock Tower, standing in the area formerly called Jisenji-no-hana, was built by the Hiroshima Rijo Lions Club, and dedicated on October 28, 1967, commemorating the tenth anniversary of their charter. They decided to build it in cooperation with the preservation movement for the A-bomb Dome. The Peace Clock Tower was made with the hope that its chime would say to the world "No More Hiroshimas" at 8:15 every day, the time when mankind first experienced the A-bomb, and with the hope that a lasting peace for all mankind can soon be established.

Peace Clock Tower

(20) Peace Fountain The Peace Fountain is located near the Children's Peace Monument. On September 1, 1960, it was constructed to commemorate the tenth anniversary of the founding of the Hiroshima Junior Chamber of Commerce. Along the Hon River west of this fountain, students of various middle schools were engaged in the work of removing buildings when the bomb fell, killing most of them. These badly wounded children cried out for water as they lay dying. This fountain is dedicated to these dead brothers and sisters of the members of the Hiroshima Junior Chamber of Commerce.

Peace Fountain

As it supplies water for its visitors it witnesses to the value of peace. Built of Ōya stone, it sends out pure water from a lion's head on the left side.

(21) Peace Cairn The Peace Cairn, beside the Children's Peace Monument, is built of stone quarried from Mt. Ben Nevis (1,346 meters high), the highest peak in Britain. The desire for international peace is expressed in the inscription on the cairn. Mt. Ben Nevis has been known as a mountain for peace ever since a young Englishman constructed a peace memorial there on the day World War II ended in 1945. The Peace Cairn was donated by the British cities of Dudley and Fort William, in return for a memorial plaque "May the tragedy of Hiroshima become the foundation of world peace" given by the Hiroshima Junior Chamber of Commerce. It has seven local Hiroshima

Peace Cairn

stones arranged in the shape of the Hiroshima delta with two stone plaques in the center with the English inscription:

> The youth of Fort William,
> SCOTLAND
> and DUDLEY, WORCESTERSHIRE,
> ENGLAND
> who have themselves
> been linked in friendship for many years,
> have presented this stone to the youth of
> HIROSHIMA
> as a symbol of goodwill and desire for
> reconciliation and world peace.
> 1972
>
> ---
>
> This particular stone was hewn from
> Britain's highest mountain
> BEN NEVIS
> FORT WILLIAM, SCOTLAND

The monument was unveiled on August 2, 1972.

(22) Statue of a Prayer for Peace

The Statue of a Prayer for Peace stands west of and behind the Memorial Cenotaph. The unveiling ceremony took place on August 2, 1977. The figures of a mother and a child, 1.4 meters high, are placed on top of a 1.8-meter-high pedestal. The figures of a mother and a child were made and offered by Katsuzo Entsuba and the pedestal was built with money sent by students from all over Japan and by the Hiroshima Chamber of Commerce. A child held by his mother is playing the trumpet, with a crescent moon in the foreground. At the unveiling ceremony, the sculptor Katsuzo Entsuba described the meaning of his creation. "From parent to child, not yesterday but tomorrow, the crescent moon will become a full moon. . I want to sound the trumpet for peace in the search for a new future."

Statue of a Prayer for Peace

Beside this statue, there stands a monument where the poem "Dedicated to the Statue of a Prayer for Peace (August, 1978)" by a poet, Shinpei Kusano is engraved.

(23) Statue of Mother and Child in the Storm

The Statue of Mother and Child in the Storm is located on the greenbelt in front of the A-bomb Memorial Museum. The bronze statue represents a mother holding an infant tightly in her right arm and protecting another child with her left arm, leaning forward, determined to survive what-

Statue of Mother and Child in the Storm

ever suffering may confront her. It was erected on August 5, 1960, by the Hiroshima Municipal Federation of Women's Associations and is a bronze replica of an original work by Shin Hongō which was presented to the city of Hiroshima by the Japan Council Against A- and H-bombs at the time of the fifth World Conference Against A- and H-bombs.

(24) Monument of the A-bombed Teachers and Students of National Elementary Schools

This monument is situated on the greenbelt south of the International Conference Center Hiroshima. The Hiroshima A-bombed Teachers' Association took the lead in the construction of the monument. The bronze statue sculptured by Ei Akutagawa, and unveiled on August 6, 1971, represents an A-bombed woman teacher holding a pupil and looking up at the sky in desperation. The names of 774 students and 131 teachers who died in the bombing were inscribed on the day the monument was unveiled. It is estimated that 2,000 students and 200 teachers were killed by the A-bomb. There are still many teachers and students unidentified.

Monument of the A-bombed Teachers and Students of National Elementary Schools

The statue on the stone pedestal, on which a tanka (a Japanese poem of thiety-one syllables) written by an A-bomb poet, Shinoe Shōda, is written, is 2.4 meters high. The tanka is,

> The heavy bone must be a teacher,
> The small skulls beside it students
> gathered around.

The student representatives who took part in the unveiling ceremony pledged that they would link their hands in a great circle of world peace, and offered chrysanthemums, lilies, and folded cranes in front of the monument.

(25) Statue of Peace "new leaves"

The Statue of Peace "new leaves" stands on the greenbelt south of the International Conference Center Hiroshima. Erected by the Hiroshima South District Rotary Club on May 10, 1966, to commemorate the tenth anniversary of its founding, the 1.8-meter-high bronze statue sculptured by Katsuzō Entsuba represents a girl with a young deer taking a walk in a May breeze. A tanka (poem) by Dr. Hideki Yukawa, the Nobel Prize winner, is inscribed on the pedestal.

Statue of Peace "new leaves"

O god of evil, do not come this way again.
This place is reserved for those who pray for peace.

(26) Flower Clock

The flower Clock, located on the south side of the City Auditorium, was completed on June 1, 1973. The machinery of the clock was donated by the Citizen Clock Corporation and the framework was completed at municipal expense. The clockface is 6 meters across with a 2-meter-long hour hand, a 2.8-meter-long minute hand and a 2.9-meter-long second hand. The control clock is built in and the hands are run by a motor. The clock is raised 15 degrees toward the cenotaph so that it can be read easily.

Flower Clock

Seasonal flowers and plants make the clockface beautiful throughout the year. (This flower clock was removed temporarily in October, 1986 due to construction of the International Conference Center Hiroshima.)

(27) Peace Tower

The Peace Tower located on the greenbelt to the south of the Peace Memorial Hall was erected on October 30, 1974, by the Hiroshima Prefectural Committee for the Erection of a Tower to Commemorate Hiroshima's Declaration of Itself as a World Federalist City. That declaration had been made in 1954. The tower is a graceful structure of five sides which symbolize the five continents. The front side is of brown granite, the others of Grecian marble. The tower was designed by Masami Kawamura.

Peace Tower

(28) Monument Dedicated to Sankichi Tōge

This monument stands on the greenbelt north of the Peace Memorial Hall. It was built through the combined efforts of the Hiroshima Culture Council and the Construction Committee for a Monument to Sankichi Tōge, and unveiled on August 6, 1963. On the concrete base inlaid with black gems and stones, there is a trapezoidal black granite block, 70 centimeters high, 110 centimeters wide, and 50 centimeters thick, on the front of which is carved a poem by Sankichi Tōge, handwritten by Kazuko Miyake as well as

Monument Dedicated to Sankichi Tōge

an English translation of the poem by Miyao Ōhara on the back.

When the bomb fell Sankichi Tōge was in his house in Midori-machi. In the ruins of the city he carried on literary activities through a youth movement, publishing a poetry magazine as well as collections of poems. In August, 1951, he sent his *A-bomb Poetry* as a representative work of Japan to the Berlin Peace Conference, which created a great sensation all over the world. He died at the age of thirty-six on March 10, 1953.

> Give Back the Human
>
> Give back my father, give back my mother;
> Give grandpa back, grandma back;
> Give me my sons and daughters back.
>
> Give me back myself.
> Give back the human race.
> As long as this life lasts, this life,
> Give back peace
> That will never end.
>
> by Sankichi Tōge

(29) Monument of the Former Zaimoku-chō

The Monument of the Former Zaimoku-chō made of natural stone is located north of the Peace Memorial Hall where Zaimoku-chō used to be. Zaimoku-chō was about 450 meters from the hypocenter and was instantly and completely destroyed. As seen in its name, Zaimoku-chō, this was an area of lumber wholesale stores during the era of feudal government. Zaimoku-chō took pride in its glorious history and traditions. During World War II, it was included in the area in which buildings were to be demolished. At the time of the bombing, approximately 540 first and second year high school girls were engaged in the demolition work. Since the area was so close to the hypocenter the girls were all either knocked flat or blown away. These young girls, most of whom were only 13 or 14 years old, were sacrificed to the A-bomb. Some girls who could somehow manage to walk tried to escape to the nearby rivers, the Motoyasu River and the Hon River, finding their way through piles of the dead and seriously wounded. Most of them, however, fell

Monument of the Former Zaimoku-chō

dead on the way. Chased by the raging fires, they jumped into rivers and fire cisterns and were roasted by the heat. They ran about trying to escape and then finally gave up and died. Some girls who managed to get to the riverbanks were picked up by rescue boats sent out by the army and some of them were taken to camps in Ninoshima, but they all eventually died.

This monument was erected on August 6, 1957, by former residents of Zaimoku-chō who had evacuated from the city, remembering their neighborhood with fond recollections, and praying for the peace of the souls of the victims.

(30) Monument of the Former North Tenjin-chō Area

This monument stands where the destroyed Tenjin-chō used to be. Building demolition work was being carried out on that day and the dropping of the A-bomb cost many lives. According to a man who went to look for his family in the evening of August 6, the area was still burning so furiously even at six o'clock that he could not enter it.

Monument of the Former North Tenjin-chō Area

This monument was built in 1973 by those who remembered their old neighborhood with prayers for the repose of the souls of the victims. On the front of the monument is written, "August 6, 1945", and the names of the victims of the former Tenjin-chō are carved on the plate placed upon the stone.

(31) Monument to the Employees of the Hiroshima Post Office

This monument is located near where the old post office stood on the eastern end of the Motoyasu Bridge. The monument was erected on March 26, 1976, to preserve forever the site of the Hiroshima Post Office which suffered the A-bomb attack. On the front of the monument, which is made of Bluestone from Shikoku, "Monument built for those who died on duty. 288 officers of the Hiroshima Post Office killed in the atomic bombing," is engraved.

Monument to the Employees of the Hiroshima Post Office

Another monument to the employees of the Hiroshima Post Office was erected in the precincts of the Tamonin, located in Hijiyama Park, on August 6, 1953.

(32) Monument of the Hiroshima Gas Corporation

The Monument of the Hiroshima Gas Corporation built in memory of its employees killed in the atomic bombing was erected on August 2, 1967, on the riverside greenbelt (east bank of the Motoyasu River), site of its former headquarters. This cylindrical monument made of black granite is about 2 meters high and 1 meter in diameter. Five gas lamps on the top of the monument are kept burning, emitting a yellow light. The old company building with three stories above and one under the ground was a stately building made of reinforced concrete and brick. Being located 250 meters from the hypocenter, it was completely destroyed except for the southwestern corner of the building.

Monument of the Hiroshima Gas Corporation

(33) Monument to the Employees of the Coal Control-Related Company

This monument stands in the corner of the children's park along the Motoyasu River where the old company building stood at the time of the bombing. It is popularly called the A-bomb Jizō (Japanese guardian deity of children) Of the 77 employees of the company, only one woman survived. The surviving employee praying for the repose of the souls of her colleagues, appealed to people in coal-related businesses from Hokkaido to northern Kyushu, and took up a collection for erection of a monument.

The monument was completed in August, 1957. The 1.5-meter-high stone Jizō made by Kōnan Hanami stands on a lotus-shaped base which is placed upon a 1.2-meter-high pedestal. This stone is a "Hon-Komatsu stone" quarried from Mt. Ashigara in Sōshū (presently Kanagawa Prefecture). Inside the monument there is a copper plate on which the names of the victims are inscribed.

Monument to the Employees of the Coal Control-Related Company

(34) Monument for the A-Bomb Victims From the Hiroshima Agricultural Association

The Monument for the A-Bomb Victims from the Hiroshima Agricultural Association is placed on the greenbelt along the Motoyasu River where the Agricultural Association had a branch office at the time of the bombing. Some 40 workers from this branch which was located near the hypocenter, and 14 from the main office in Kokutaiji-chō were killed by the A-bomb. Many others died later. To pray for the repose of the souls of the victims, the Hiroshima Central Agricultural Cooperative Association and its related four federations erected a monument with the names of 82 victims carved on it.

Monument for the A-bomb Victims from the Hiroshima Agricultural Association

The monument made of black granite is 2 meters high and 4 meters wide. Its epigraph was written by Hisato Oku, the president of the Agricultural Association at that time. The inscription was selected by Mr. Yukihiro, the chairman of the Dōeisha Cooperative Federation. And the inscription and the names of the 82 victims were handwritten by Mr. Itō, the chairman of the Hiroshima Central Agricultural Cooperative Association. The monument was unveiled on July 31, 1971.

(35) Hair Monument

The Hair Monument is located on the greenbelt along the Motoyasu River. It was erected in March 1960, by the Hiroshima Barbers' Association. It was built by Yutaka Ikeda. It contains a brief poem,

We enshrine here hair,
Cut and gathered in the morn of life.

The monument is a prayer for the advancement of the barbering profession and an expression of gratitude.

Hair Monument

(36) Mobilized Students' Merciful Kannon Monument

The Mobilized Students' Merciful Kannon Monument was erected for the worship of the souls of the students who were killed by the A-bomb. The monument is located on the greenbelt along the Motoyasu River. Interested persons of the bereaved families of the students who came from twenty-one middle schools and girls' schools of the old system in Hiroshima, took the initiative in building this monument. It was erected on July 31, 1966. About 4,000 names of the dead are engraved on the copper nameplate which is 30 centimeters long and 50 centimeters wide. The nameplate is stored

Mobilized Students' Merciful Kannon Monument

in the base of the monument. A 2-meter-high bronze statue of Kannon is erected on the base. Hōko Sunahara built the monument.

There are two poems engraved in marble on the base.

"In reverence for the spirits of these students
Who have become Kannons preserving peace."
Yasuo Yamamoto

"We find peace in thinking of you
Sleeping in the arms of the merciful Kannon."
Reisuke Masuda

The number of students killed by the A-bomb was presumed to be about 6,000. As soon as the names of others become known they will be added to the nameplate.

(37) A-Bomb Monument of the Hiroshima Municipal Girls' High School

The A-Bomb Monument of the Hiroshima Municipal Girls' High School is erected on the greenbelt at the western edge of the Peace Bridge. The annihilation of the first and second graders of this school, who were mobilized for the demolition of buildings, has been described in the paragraph on the monument of Zaimoku-chō. This monument was originally erected on the campus of their school in 1948, but when their school was abolished because of changes in the school system, it was moved to its present location on June 20, 1957.

A-bomb Monument of the Hiroshima Municipal Girls' High School

The monument consists of a 2-meter-high block of stone with the image of a high school girl in her working uniform engraved on the front. It was designed by the sculptor Kenyū Kouchiyama. On one side of the student a friend is offering a wreath of flowers, symbolizing reverence for her memory, on the other side a friend is offering a dove, symbolizing peace. The student in the center is holding a box with "$E = MC^2$" engraved on it, symbolizing atomic energy.

On the back of the stone there is a poem by Zōroku Miyagawa who was principal of the school at the time of the bombing.

"Rest in peace within this grassy hill
Protected by a wall of friends.
August 6, 1948. Masaomi Miyagawa"

Since the erection of memorial monuments was prohibited under the

Allied Occupation, this monument was erected as a peace monument.

(38) Monument of the Former South Tenjin-chō Area

The Monument of the Former South Teinjin-chō Area stands on the greenbelt west of the Peace Bridge. This community was completely destroyed by the A-bomb. The disaster was utterly beyond description. Those who were at home and those outside engaged in the demolition of buildings were all killed instantly. Some friends who had ties to the community decided to have a memorial monument built. It was erected on October 15, 1973.

Monument of the Former South Tenjin-chō Area

The monument is made of granite with a copper plaque of three dancing heavenly maidens. It was designed by Masanami Yoshida of the Hijiyama Junior College Art Department, and made by Itō-Kyuhodo. The Tenmangu (shrine), popular among the townspeople, was located in this community; not being one of the buildings to be removed, it was destroyed by the A-bomb explosion.

(39) Friendship Monument

This monument on the greenbelt immediately south of the Peace Park across the Peace Boulevard was built by the Hiroshima District Council of the Japan Association of Casualty Insurance Underwriters on August 3, 1965. This monument is dedicated to the 89 employees of the Hiroshima branch of the Tokyo Marine Fire Insurance Association and the member companies of the Japan Association of Casualty Insurance Underwriters. This marble monument is 2.4 meters high and was designed by Shindō Tsuji of the Kyoto Municipal Art College. The four crosses on top of the column symbolize human bodies. "Four" represents four continents: the whole world. The four human bodies thus represent the conscience of love of all people who long for peace.

Friendship Monument

(40) Memorial Monument for the Hiroshima Municipal Commercial School

The Hiroshima Municipal Commercial School became the Hiroshima Municipal Shipbuilding Technical School near the end of World War II, but after the war, the school began again as the Hiroshima Municipal Commercial High School. The memorial monument of this school is located at the west end of the

Peace Park with the Hon River behind it. The monument is a combination of huge natural stones. On the top of the stone lying in front, "Memorial Monument" is carved in a vigorous style. On the back of it is inscribed:

Memorial Monument for the Hiroshima Municipal Commercial School

"It was exactly like a thunderbolt from the clear sky. At 8:15 on August 6, 1945, our hometown Hiroshima was demolished in an instant by a single atomic bomb, becoming a hell on earth. Our school had been compelled to change into a shipbuilding school, but on that day the 270 students who were on duty performing demolition work in the city along with three members of the school staff were all killed.

Your experience is so sad and pitiful that we do not know what to say to you, you who were young and had such a noble patriotic concern for our country. We herein pray for the repose of your souls and give our pledge that such a tragedy shall not be repeated by human hands.

We also remember the souls of the graduates of our school who died so bravely in battle in this war and have become guardian spirits of our country. May this stone preserve our feelings for many generations. August 6, 1963. The Alumni Association of the Hiroshima Municipal Commercial School, the Bereaved Families of the Shipbuilding Technical School. Kōzō Tanaka, Principal of the Hiroshima Commercial High School."

As already described, at the time of the explosion 270 students and 3 teachers were at work removing houses near the prefectural office building (in Kako-machi). They were all killed. Later on the students' lunch boxes and unburnt pieces of their clothes were found. However, their ashes could not be identified. Some of the students jumped into the nearby Hon River and died there.

(41) Hiroshima Second Middle School A-Bomb Memorial Monument

The Hiroshima 2-nd Middle School A-bomb Memorial Monument stands on the Hon River by the International Conference Center Hiroshima. When the students were removing houses on the riverbank, they were exposed to the A-bomb, and many were

Hiroshima Second Middle School A-bomb Memorial Monument

killed. There is a dirge,

> "As we think of your faces and deeds there are no words. We can only weep,"

carved on thr front of the monument which is made of a large natural stone. On the back of it is carved: "Ah, August 6, 1945. Seven teachers and 343 students have died in the atomic blast and become the cornerstone of peace. Built on August 6, 1953, by the bereaved families of the Hiroshima 2nd Middle School."

(42) Monument for the Volunteer Army Corps

This monument stands on the greenbelt near the Honkawa Bridge, dedicated on August 6, 1964, by the bereaved families of the volunteer army corps which was organized in Nukui, Kawauchi Village, Satō-chō, Asa County. All the members of the volunteer army corps of Nukui were exposed to the A-bomb and killed while demolishing buildings. They were all males whose families depended on them for support. Thus this morning brought the village a tragedy and it became a village with no men. The whole village was stunned and thrown into confusion. The following is written: "Dedicated respectfully to the memory of those in the volunteer army corps. We will not forget that tragic day. At 8:15 on August 6, 1945, an A-bomb was dropped on this place. In the pit of hell our beloved ones suffered agony and entered their final sleep. Though it was the supreme order of the military, it resulted in the sacrifice of 174 lives. They were called the Kawauchi Village Volunteers, all residents of the Nukui Community in Kawauchi Village, Asa County. We who loved you vow that peace will be built, beginning in this place. We are proud of your great sacrifice and will remember it forever. Rest in peace."

Monument for the Volunteer Army Corps

(43) Monument in Memory of the Korean Victims of the A-Bomb

The Monument in Memory of the Korean Victims of the A-Bomb was erected by the Hiroshima Headquarters of the South Korean Residents of Japan on April 10, 1970. It is located on the greenbelt at the western edge of the Honkawa Bridge. A tower stands on a large turtle-shaped base with the epigraph "Monument in Memory of the Korean Victims of the A-Bomb: Prince Lee-Woo and 20,000 others". At the top of the tower there is a crown engraved with two dragons in which the names of the bombing victims are stored. Korean stones were used for the monument, which was produced in the Republic of Korea and later transported to this place. It is about 5 meters high and weighs about 10 tons.

Monument in Memory of the Korean Victims of the A-bomb

The Prince Lee-Woo mentioned in the inscription was a nephew of Prince Lee-Eun, the last Korean crown Prince. He was a staff officer in education at the time of the bombing, attached to the Command Headquarters with the Fifth Cavalry which was quarters in Futabanosato. He was on his way to work on horseback from his quarters in the Maeda villa in Takasu, Furuta-chō, and was near the Aioi Bridge when the bomb exploded. Although he was taken to the temporary first-aid station on Ninoshima by a relief squad of the Akatsuki Unit, he died the next day. The monument was erected at this site because it was near the place where Prince Lee-Woo was found.

It is said that between 30,000 and 40,000 Korean people, those who were residents of the city and those who were brought to Japan from the Korean Peninsula as forced labor, were in Hiroshima at the time of the bombing.

Flowers and Trees in the Peace Park

The whole area of the Peace Park, situated as it was near the hypocenter, was instantly flattened with a great number of people killed instantly. Before shacks were built the area was overgrown with grass. Horseweed as tall as a man waved in the wind. In the midst of the grass, grave-posts of plain wood were set up here and there. Where the largest grave-post stood, there is now a low grassy mound, the cairn for the victims of the bomb. One hibakusha who used to live beside the A-bomb Dome planted a camphor tree there to symbolize his hope for the reconstruction of the city. It has now grown large and has luxuriant foliage. Immediately after the park area was cleared, trees were planted. In addition to the planned tree planting by the city, a great number of trees and flowers were sent by individuals and groups both inside and outside Japan, who wanted to remember the souls of the victims and pray for peace. Thus the present woods in the park was formed.

Flowers and Trees in the Peace Park

For example, on April 18, 1961, the Hiroshima branch of the New

Japan Council conducted a nation-wide campaign to donate trees and they received 200, representing the prefectures of Japan. A square black-granite monument was set up south of the City Auditorium commemorating this occasion. Also in the park there are some 400 cherry trees, either donated by, or in memory of, various groups. The park presents a lively scene every year as people enjoy the cherry blossoms.

(44) Mounment for the "Woods of Peace"

The letters "Woods of Peace" inscribed on the monument are in the handwriting of Takayuki Takagi, chairman of the Hiroshima Association for the "Woods of Peace." Its monument was constructed in commemoration of the Peace Memorial National Festival which the Association initiated in 1960.

Tree-Planting Ceremony at the Monument for the "Woods of Peace"

(45) Monument of "Zensonpo" (All Japan Nonlife Insurance Labor Union)

There is an old cycad tree in the greenbelt at the southern corner in front of the Peace Memorial Hall.

In front of the cycad there is a square stone monument on which is carved: "Why did that day happen? Why does it continue? Do not forget that hatred and this vow."

This monument was erected by the All Japan Nonlife Insurance Labor Union on August 6, 1965, commemorating the 20th anniversary of the A-bomb.

Monument for the "Woods of Peace"

There are also three phoenix trees, situated north of the hall, which were exposed to the A-bomb while they stood in the garden of the Post and Telegraphic Service Office in Hakushima-chō. Though the surfaces of the trunks of these trees facing the hypocenter were burnt, they survived and were transplanted here in 1972. Thus there are many flowers and trees in the park which have their own historical background. As for the flowers and trees from abroad, there are European oaks planted in memory of a visit to Hiroshima by German university professors in 1961, roses sent by the British Government as an expression of friendship,

Monument of "Zensonpo" (All Japan Nonlife Insurance Labor Union)

also roses contributed by the Albert Schweitzer Society in Amsterdam, Holland in 1971, Washington coconut plams sent from Hawaii to commemorate the ties between Hiroshima and Honolulu as sister cities in 1959, Himalayan cedars planted to commemorate the visit of the former prime minister of India, Jawaharlal Nehru, in 1957, and many other memorial trees. These flowers and trees are fitting symbols in a park dedicated to international peace.

Doves as Symbols of Peace

There are approximately 4,000 to 5,000 doves in the Peace Park. On August 6, 1949, the Peace Memorial Ceremony was observed on a makeshift stage at the place where the municipal baseball stadium is presently located, to commemorate the enactment of the law to reconstruct Hiroshima as a Peace City. On that occasion, white doves were released from a decorative paper ball opened by hibakusha with the vow "No More Hiroshimas." This was the first time that doves were released in the Peace Memorial Ceremony.

Doves as Symbols of Peace

In 1959, about 80 doves, as a symbol of peace, were collected by the Hiroshima branch of the Japan Pigeon Racing Association, and donated to the city. They have multiplied year by year and now form a large family. However, the park gradually become too crowded for the doves, and some of them have gone to other places, such as the woods on the site of the Hiroshima Castle and the park at Hijiyama where they have formed new groups. Among the doves released every year on the occasion of the Peace Memorial Ceremony, there seem to be some who do not return to their owners but settle down in the park with the others.

(46) Hiroshima City Zero Milestone

The zero milestone of Hiroshima City is located on the eastern edge of the Motoyasu Bridge. The distance from Hiroshima City to other places used to be measured with this milestone as the starting point. Until the A-bomb was dropped on the city, it stood in front of the Hiroshima Post Office which was then situated about 30 meters to the east of the present milestone. It was burnt by the intense thermal rays of the A-bomb and its corners were broken off. It was probably erected when Hiroshima

Hiroshima City Zero Milestone

officially became a city in 1889.

(47) Monument in Memory of Dr. Marcel Junod

A Swiss doctor, the late Dr. Marcel Junod came to Hiroshima on September 8, 1945 when the A-bomb tragedy still filled the city. Dr. Junod, as Chief Representative to Japan of the International Red Cross Committee came with the Allied Forces investigating team led by Thomas Farrel, bringing 15 tons of medicine which was provided by the General Headquarters of the Occupation Forces. He remained in Hiroshima even after the team withdrew, and made his best efforts to help the A-bomb survivors.

Monument in Memory of Dr. Marcel Junod

To honor his work and love for humanity, the monument was erected on September 8, 1979 at the southern entrance of the Peace Memorial Park. The monument is made of black granite in the shape of a cross, 1.2 meters high and 1.6 meters wide. On the front of the monument are a relief of Dr. Junod and the following words, in English and Japanese: "On August 9, 1945, Dr. Marcel Junod arrived in this country as Chief Representative to Japan of the International Red Cross Committee. On hearing of the terrible destruction caused by the atomic bombing in Hiroshima, Dr. Junod immediately proceeded to the General Headquarters of the Occupation Forces and insisted that the authorities send relief medicine to Hiroshima. On September 8, he entered the devastated city with no less than fifteen tons of prepared medicines. While occupied in surveying the actual extent of the appaling catastrophe, he himself treated many citizens who had fallen victim to the A-bomb. The medicines brought to the city through his endeavors were distributed to each aid station, saving thousands of A-bomb survivors. We erect this monument in grateful remembrance of Dr. Junod for his humane acts and as a tribute to the International Red Cross for its continuing work of human compassion." On the back of the monument, the words of Dr. Junod are carved as follows: "Innumerable cries are asking for your help."

The monument was erected by the Committee to Erect a Monument to Dr. Junod, with 8 million yen which the committee raised.

(48) Hiroshima Monument for the A-bomb Victims

On August 5, 1982, the Hiroshima Monument for the A-bomb Victims was dedicated in the green belt on the riverbank opposite the Peace Memorial Park. The monument is the result of a devoted campaign carried out by the Executive Committee of the Hiroshima High School Student Peace Seminar (headed by Chairman Hiroki Kōno, 3rd year student at Sōtoku High School). They excavated roof tiles from the bombing from the bed of the Motoyasu River and appealed to the public for their preservation.

Hiroshima Monument for the A-bomb Victims

The monument consists of a bronze statue standing on a pedestal. The pedestal is 3 meters wide, 1.5 meters high and 0.7 meters deep. The statue is the work of Ei Akutagawa, professor at Hijiyama Women's Junior College. It is supposed to depict the souls of A-bomb victims ascending to Heaven. On the front of the pedestal there is a panel of the A-bomb tiles with an epitaph. On the back are a relief depicting the excavation work, a picture taken immediately after the A-bomb explosion, and a ceramic tablet with an explanation in English and Japanese. The epitaph reads: "When the sky turned suddenly light, my body began to melt. Friends around the world, join in the cry from Hiroshima!"

(49) Monument Commemorating Pope John Paul II's Appeal for Peace

On February 25, 1981, Pope John Paul II made an appeal for the total abolition of nuclear arms in his "Appeal for Peace" before the A-bomb Cenotaph in the Peace Park. His appeal greatly impressed people all over the world.

Monument Commemorating Pope John Paul II's Appeal for Peace

The appeal of a hibakusha, Yoshie Fujieda to erect a monument commemorating his visit to Hiroshima, and making his peace appeal a foundation for world peace, brought about the organizing of the Committee for Erecting a Memorial Monument (chairman: Tōmin Harada). As the result of a fund-raising campaign the monument was erected and the Unveiling ceremony took place on February 25, 1983 in the first-floor lobby of the Hiroshima Peace Memorial Hall with the participation of Archbishop Mario Pio Gaspari of the Papal Court, Mayor Araki and some 150 others.

The monument is an abstract sculpture from two pieces of stone symbolizing a future of harmony and stability throughout the world. It expresses the hope of the people of the world for peace. The monument is 3 meters high, 1.8 meters wide and 0.9 meters deep. It is made of white marble from Carrara, Italy by a sculptor from Hiroshima, presently living in Italy, Kazuto Kuetani. The committee raised 4 million yen in donations for the erection of this monument.

The inscription was selected from the Pope's "Peace Appeal" and appears in both English and Japanese (the calligraphy was done by Hiromu Morishita). "War is the work of man. War is destruction of human life. War is death. To remember the past is to commit oneself to the future. To remember Hiroshima is to abhor nuclear war. To remember Hiroshima is to commit oneself to peace."

(50) Prayer Monument for Peace

Prayer Monument for Peace

The record downpour which struck the prefecture of Nagasaki on July 23, 1982, left 299 dead or missing, of which 262 were from Nagasaki City. Having learned of the disaster, the Hiroshima Nishi Lions Club (Keizo Yoshino President) sent contributions for relief to the Nagasaki Nishi Lions Club (Hidenori Harada President). This led the two Lions Clubs to become sister clubs on March 23, 1983, and they decided to erect similar monuments for peace in Hiroshima and Nagasaki in commemoration of this relationship with hopes for the abolition of nuclear weapons and for eternal peace. Each Lions Club donated 3 million yen to build the monuments. Unveiling ceremonies took place on February 11, 1984, in Nagasaki and on June 24, the same year in Hiroshima.

The Hiroshima monument, which is 1.7 meters high and made of granite, stands in the green belt on the east bank of the Motoyasu River. The moument consists of two granite slabs connected by a horizontal granite bar with an inscription in Mayor Araki's handwriting, supporting a globe, 40cm in diameter. The monument's message is carved in Japanese on the right slab and in English on the left with a flying dove on both stones:

> The Lions Clubs of Hiroshima and Nagasaki,
> sister cities, having experienced the tragedy
> of atomic bombing, erect this monument as
> a symbol of eternal peace for mankind.
>
> March 14, 1984
> Calligraphy by
> Mayor of Hiroshima
>
> The International Association of Lions Clubs
> District 336-C The Hiroshima Nishi Lions Club

The monument is dated March 14, 1984, because this was the anniversary of the day on which the Hiroshima Nishi Lions Club was organized.

(51) Prayer Haiku Monument for Peace

Carved on this monument is a haiku by former prime minister, Yasuhiro Nakasone, expressing his deep emotions at the time he attended the 1983 Hiroshima Peace Memorial Ceremony. It reads: "Toward the summer clouds, full of sorrow, doves are set free." (The calligraphy is Nakasone's.) Former prime minister Nakasone attended the Peace Memorial Ceremony three times in Hiroshima and twice in Nagasaki while he was in office. To express Nakasone's feelings for the victims of the A-bombing and his wish for peace, the Association of People from Hiroshima Prefecture, Tokyo Chapter suggested that the Hiroshima Futaba Lions Club (Shigeyoshi Odoriba President) erect a monument with Nakasone's haiku.

Prayer Haiku Monument for Peace

The Hiroshima Futaba Lions Club decided to build the monument on September 25, 1987, and erected it on November 12, 1987. The monument stands in the green belt on the east bank of the Motoyasu River. The monument is made of stones in the shape of the Chinese character meaning "human being" on paving stones which also form the same Chinese character. The monument was designed by volunteers trying to convey to future generations the pain of those who perished in the A-bombing.

(52) A-Bombed Gravestone

This ruin was the gravestone of Kunai Okamoto, a senior statesman of the Asano Clan (which was in control of the Hiroshima area at that time.)

The gravestone was located in Jisenji temple (38 Nakajima-hon-machi, Hiroshima) approximately 200 meters from the hypocenter.

The top of the gravestone was blown off and destroyed by the tremendous blast.

A-Bombed Gravestone

Stone Lantern of Peace

(53) Stone Lantern of Peace

This Stone Lantern of Peace was constructed on August 6, 1955 by the Tankokai Hiroshima branch of the Urasenke Tea Ceremony School to pray for the peace of the souls of the A-bomb victims. On the side of the pedestal a plaque was attached in 1977 which reads, "A poem written on the occasion of the 33rd Anniversary of the A-bombing" by Tanshosai Ishii, the head of the Tankokai Hiroshima branch. The poem reads, "Praying for the repose of the souls of those who fell victim, this pedestal is made in the shape of a tatami (straw-mat) so that in prayer tea can be offered throughout the year in quiet peace as guests are received in harmony." Each year on August 6, tea is offered before this Stone Lantern of Peace.

(54) Monument dedicated to Construction Workers and Artisans

Monument dedicated to Construction Workers and Artisans

The Atomic bombs dropped on Hiroshima August 6 and on Nagasaki August 9, 1945 inflicted a great many casualties on construction workers and artisans as well as their families. In order to comfort the souls of these A-bomb victims and to pass on the message that no nation or race should fall victim again, 430,000 members of the All Japan Construction Workers Union agreed upon construction of monuments in Hiroshima and Nagasaki.

The monument in Hiroshima was erected and unveiled on August 5, 1988. The monument in Hiroshima stands in the greenbelt on the east riverbank of the Motoyasu River. On the front of the monument the words "Rest in peace. Monument to A-bombed construction workers and artisans," are carved. The inscription on the back of the monument reads, "The 430,000 members of the All Japan Construction Workers are united in erecting this monument praying for the repose of the souls of the A-bombed workers and their families, and wishing to abolish all nuclear weapons from the earth and to create a peaceful and fruitful world. August 5, 1988. All Japan Construction Workers Union and Hiroshima Prefecture Construction Workers Union." The monument is made of granite in the shape of a house roof, 1.1 meters high, 1.4 meters wide and 1 meter deep.

(55) & (56) Peace Bridge and West Peace Bridge

Peace Bridge

The Peace Bridge spanning the Motoyasu River and the West Peace Bridge across the Hon River are two unique bridges, constructed on the Peace Boulevard which runs from Hijiyama Park in the east to Nishi Hiroshima (Koi) Station in the west. The handrails of both bridges, which serve as gateways to the Peace Park, were designed by a prominant American sculptor, Isamu Noguchi, and were completed in March 1952. Among the 1,400 entries in the contest to name the bridges, "Peace Bridge" was the most frequently suggested. Twenty-six-year-old Yoshisuke Murase, who lived in Jigozen, Saeki County, won the subsequent drawing.

West Peace Bridge

The designs for the Peace Bridge (85.5 meters long and 15 meters wide) and the West Peace Bridge (101.9 meters long and 15 meters wide) perfectly symbolize the new city of Hiroshima. The former is an abstract expression of the rising sun and the latter of the setting sun. However, since the designs were quite unusual, they provoked heated discussions not only in the city assembly but even among the people of the city, who brought out various art theories to support their positions. However the designs were finally approved. Prof. Tange also lauded them saying, "They are magnificent bridges which enhance the Peace Park that I designed." Isamu Noguchi, son of Yoneiirō Noguchi, a poet, is an internationally recognized artist whose creations include the Japanese garden built for the UNESCO Headquarters in Paris. He died in 1988.

(57) & (58) Motoyasu Bridge and Honkawa Bridge

Motoyasu Bridge

When Terumoto Mōri constructed the Hiroshima Castle and established a castle town, he changed the route of the Sanyō Highway, which ran through the mountains, and routed it through the town, hoping to ensure the prosperity of his castle town. The Motoyasu

Bridge and the Honkawa Bridge were built at that time as parts of the highway.

The blast of the bomb struck the Motoyasu Bridge (50 meters long and 7 meters wide) directly from above so that the railings on both sides of the bridge were pushed outward and fell into the river. The stone lanterns on both sides of the bridge were also moved outward toward the edge of the bridge. Because of this the scientific investigation team checked the Motoyasu Bridge carefully and decided that the bomb must have been exploded directly over the bridge. The floor of the bridge itself was not heavily damaged and people continued to use it.

Honkawa Bridge

The Honkawa Bridge (73.2 meters long and 7.6 meters wide), located 250 meters from the hypocenter, was blown off its foundation by the blast and part of the bridge collapsed.

(59) Aioi Bridge

The Aioi Bridge, said to have been the target of the A-bombing, was heavily damaged. The violent blast hit the surface of the Ōta River and rebounded, lifting the sidewalk of the bridge which was made of reinforced concrete. The handrails on both sides were pushed outward and the rail on the north side fell into the river. After the war, it was temporarily repaired and used. However, on November 2, 1983, the bridge was reconstructed.

The reconstructed bridge is 123.4 meters long and 40 meters wide (the widest bridge in Hiroshima), with six traffic lanes and streetcar lines running in the middle. It also has a sidewalk on both sides that is 6 meters wide. In rebuilding the bridge, special efforts were made to keep the bridge in harmony with the Peace Park, the A-bomb Dome and surrounding area. To do so, granite was used for the handrails and the pillars. The design for the bridge symbolizes an aspiration for peace which has been the earnest desire of Hiroshima. The Aioi Bridge is unique and nationally famous for its T-shaped design with another bridge running from the middle of the main bridge to the Peace Park.

The following is a brief summary of the history of the bridge.

≪The Edo period≫ Since the building of bridges was prohibited due to political and military reasons in order to form a

Aioi Bridge

castle town, small boats were used to cross the river.

≪The Meiji period≫ Although the building of bridges was permitted in this period, the city administration was poorly funded for bridge building. In 1878, with donations from citizens, the East Aioi Bridge and the West Aioi Bridge were built of wood with Jisenji-no-hana (the northern edge of the Peace Park) as the starting point. At a hut built in Jisenji-no-hana, a crossing fee for both bridges was collected (one rin per person and three rin per cow or horse or cart. On rin equals to $\frac{1}{1000}$ yen). This fee was used for the repair of the bridges. The charging of a crossing fee was not well thought of by the citizens. However, on January 1, 1897, when the control of the bridges was transferred to the city administration, the crossing of the bridges became free of charge. Since Nakajima-cho area (around the present Peace Park) was the most flourishing quarter of Hiroshima at that time, there were a number of people who used the bridges. With the development of the city, the reclamation of the outer moat of the Hiroshima Castle, on which streetcar lines were to be laid, was completed in November 1911.

≪The Taisho period≫ On December 8, 1912, a bridge for the exclusive use of streetcars was built 50 meters north of the East and West Aioi Bridges, and streetcar service between Hiroshima Station and Koi was opened. It made travel between the two points much easier.

≪The Showa period≫ On December 11, 1932, the bridge was rebuilt of reenforced concrete for the use of both pedestrians and vehicles. On October 6, 1934, another reenforced-concrete bridge was built connecting Jisenji-no-hana to the middle of the bridge. With the East and West Aioi Bridges, which still existed at that time, the design of the bridges was H-shaped. However, the old East and West Aioi Bridges were removed in 1939. Since then, the Aioi Bridge has been T-shaped. On August 6, 1945, the bridge was heavily damaged. However, according to records, immediately after the A-bomb was dropped, rescue troops temporarily evacuated innumerable burnt corpses to the Aioi Bridge which was still passable.

1. A-bomb Cenotaph
2. Flame of Peace
3. Hiroshima Peace Memorial Hall
4. Hiroshima Peace Memorial Museum
5. Hiroshima City Auditorium
6. Fountain of Prayer
7. Children's Peace Monument
8. A-Bomb Dome
9. Literary Monument Dedicated to Miekichi Suzuki
10. Monument to the Old Aioi Bridge
11. Monument to Those Who Died From the Chūgoku-Shikoku Public Works Office
12. Monument of the Hiroshima District Lumber Control Corporation
13. Monument to Tamiki Hara
14. Memorial Tower to the Mobilized Students
15. Atomic Bomb Memorial Mound
16. Monument of Prayer
17. The Figure of the Merciful Goddess of Peace (Kannon)
18. Peace Bell
19. Peace Clock Tower
20. Peace Fountain
21. Peace Cairn
22. Statue of a Prayer for Peace
23. Statue of Mother and Child in the Storm
24. Monument of the A-bombed Teachers and Students of National Elementary Schools
25. Statue of Peace "new leaves"
26. Flower Clock (removed)
27. Peace Tower
28. Monument Dedicated to Sankichi Tōge
29. Monument of the Former Zaimoku-chō
30. Monument of the Former North Tenjin-chō Area
31. Monument to the Employees of the Hiroshima Post Office
32. Monument of the Hiroshima Gas Corporation
33. Monument to the Employees of the Coal Control-Related Company
34. Monument for the A-bomb Victims From the Hiroshima Agricultural Association
35. Hair Monument
36. Mobilized Students' Merciful Kannon Monument
37. A-bomb Monument of the Hiroshima Municipal Girls' High School
38. Monument of the Former South Tenjin-chō Area
39. Friendship Monument
40. Memorial Monument for the Hiroshima Municipal Commercial School
41. Hiroshima Second Middle School A-bomb Memorial Monument
42. Monument for the Volunteer Army Corps
43. Monument in Memory of the Korean Victims of the A-bomb
44. Monument for the "Woods of Peace"
45. Monument of "Zensonpo" (All Japan Nonlife Insurance Labor Union)
46. Hiroshima City Zero Milestone
47. Monument in Memory of Dr. Marcel Junod
48. Hiroshima Monument for the A-bomb Victims
49. Monument Commemorating Pope John Paul II's Appeal for Peace
50. Prayer Monument for Peace
51. Prayer Haiku Monument for Peace
52. A-Bombed Gravestone
53. Stone Lantern of Peace
54. Monument dedicated to Construction Workers and Artisans
55. Peace Bridge
56. West Peace Bridge
57. Motoyasu Bridge
58. Honkawa Bridge
59. Aioi Bridge

a. Map of Nakajima-hon-machi before the A-bombing
b. Phoenix Trees Exposed to the A-bomb
c. Clock Commemorating the Repatriation of Those Who Chose to Return to the Democratic People's Republic of Korea

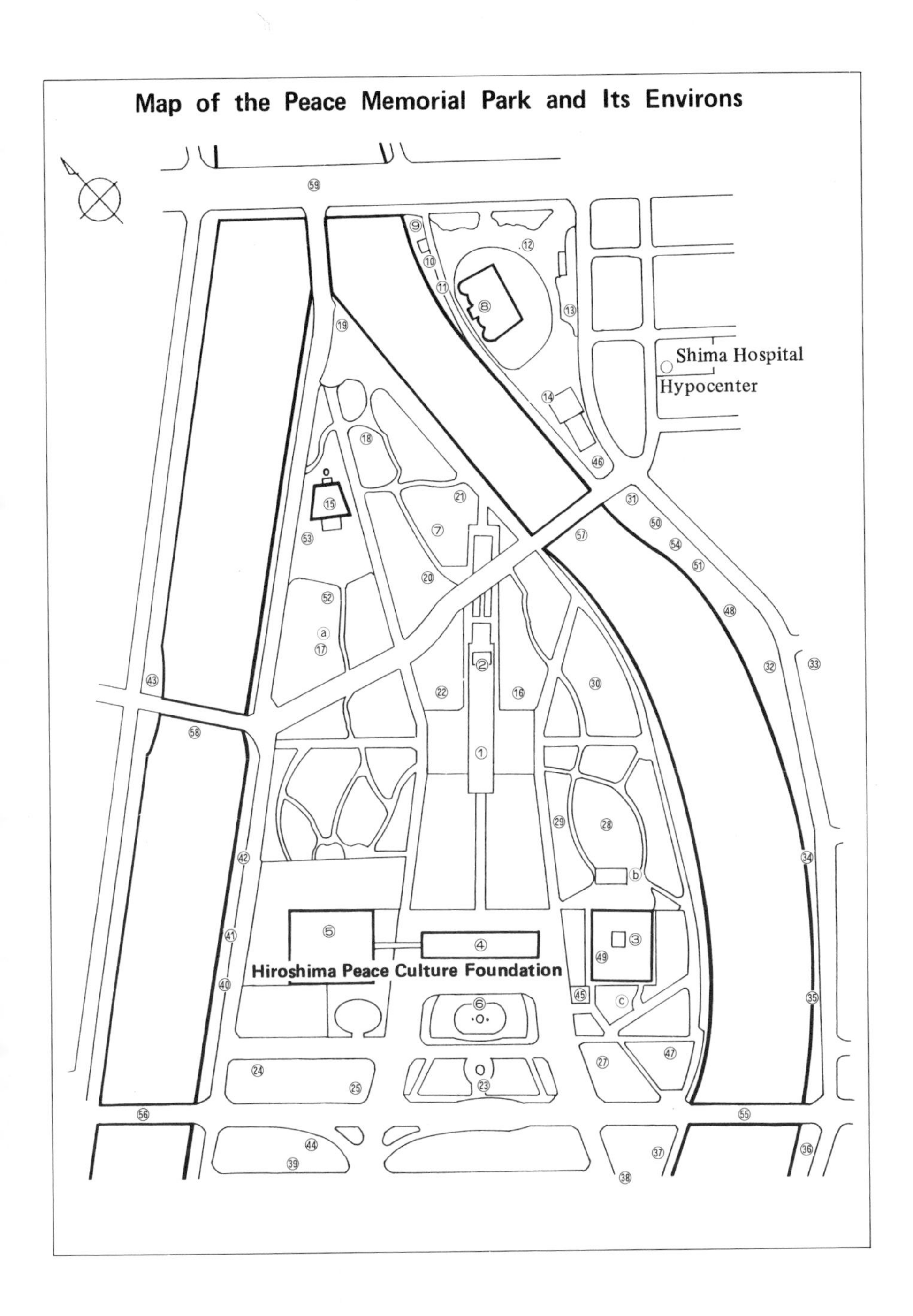
Map of the Peace Memorial Park and Its Environs
Shima Hospital
Hypocenter
Hiroshima Peace Culture Foundation

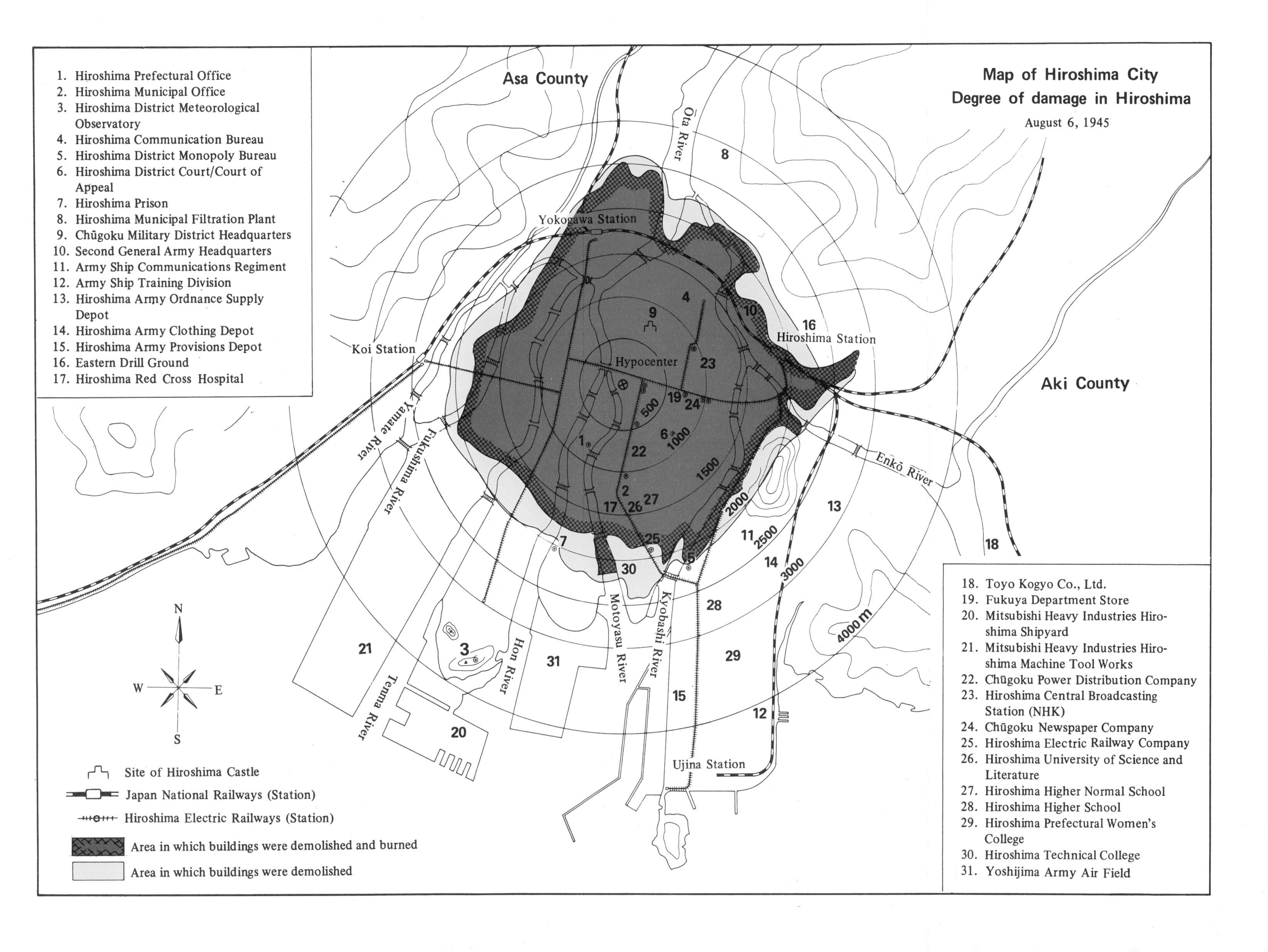

Map of Hiroshima City
Degree of damage in Hiroshima
August 6, 1945
1. Hiroshima Prefectural Office
2. Hiroshima Municipal Office
3. Hiroshima District Meteorological Observatory
4. Hiroshima Communication Bureau
5. Hiroshima District Monopoly Bureau
6. Hiroshima District Court/Court of Appeal
7. Hiroshima Prison
8. Hiroshima Municipal Filtration Plant
9. Chūgoku Military District Headquarters
10. Second General Army Headquarters
11. Army Ship Communications Regiment
12. Army Ship Training Division
13. Hiroshima Army Ordnance Supply Depot
14. Hiroshima Army Clothing Depot
15. Hiroshima Army Provisions Depot
16. Eastern Drill Ground
17. Hiroshima Red Cross Hospital
18. Toyo Kogyo Co., Ltd.
19. Fukuya Department Store
20. Mitsubishi Heavy Industries Hiroshima Shipyard
21. Mitsubishi Heavy Industries Hiroshima Machine Tool Works
22. Chūgoku Power Distribution Company
23. Hiroshima Central Broadcasting Station (NHK)
24. Chūgoku Newspaper Company
25. Hiroshima Electric Railway Company
26. Hiroshima University of Science and Literature
27. Hiroshima Higher Normal School
28. Hiroshima Higher School
29. Hiroshima Prefectural Women's College
30. Hiroshima Technical College
31. Yoshijima Army Air Field
Asa County
Aki County
Ōta River
Yokogawa Station
Koi Station
Hiroshima Station
Hypocenter
Yamate River
Fukushima River
Enkō River
Hon River
Temma River
Motoyasu River
Kyobashi River
Ujina Station
500
1000
1500
2000
2500
3000
4000 m
N
S
W
E
Site of Hiroshima Castle
Japan National Railways (Station)
Hiroshima Electric Railways (Station)
Area in which buildings were demolished and burned
Area in which buildings were demolished